# BREAKING AND TRAINING YOUR HORSE

# BREAKING AND TRAINING YOUR HORSE

## Sheila Roughton

### BHSI

WARD LOCK

## ACKNOWLEDGEMENTS

I would like to thank my father Geoffrey Chandler, not only for all his advice and encouragement during the writing of this book but also throughout my career with horses; Mary Cheney, who has spent many hours deciphering and typing the text; and Ian and Martha Shaw for providing all the photographs and the people and horses included in them. I would also like to thank Philip Surl and Christie Lomax of Rushton Hall Stables, and the many other establishments who kindly loaned their facilities for use in the photographs.

**A WARD LOCK BOOK**

First published in the UK 1994
by Ward Lock
Villiers House
41/47 Strand
LONDON
WC2N 5JE
A Cassell Imprint

Copyright Text © Sheila Roughton 1994

Distributed in the United States
by Sterling Publishing Co., Inc.
387 Park Avenue South, New York, NY 10016-8810

Distributed in Australia
by Capricorn Link (Australia) Pty Ltd
2/13 Carrington Road, Castle Hill, NSW 2154

A British Library Cataloguing in Publication Data block for this book may be obtained from the British Library

ISBN 0-7063-7123-2

Typeset by Litho Link Ltd, Welshpool, Powys, Wales
Printed and bound in Slovenia by Printing House DELO – Tiskarna
by arrangement with Korotan Italiana, Ljubljana

# CONTENTS

# FOREWORD

*Above* The formation of trust between horse and human is the basis of successful training.

*Opposite* A proud moment for both horse and rider.

Over the years, many different theories and methods have been tried in the breaking and training of horses. Some of these methods have been continued and developed, while others have been discarded. In North America the Indians used to lead an unbroken pony from an older one into a river. Two young braves would sit on the older pony until they reached deeper water, when one would slide across on to the back of the unbroken pony. Because it was standing in deep water, the pony would be unlikely to buck because it would then have to put its nose under the water. The ponies then walked and swam until the youngster was tired and then the Indians rode it out on to dry land. It was rather a hit and miss affair but nevertheless effective.

Another method, used by cowboys at about the same time, was tried during long cattle drives. The drovers would have one good horse each and several unbroken ones. These would run loose with the herd of cattle for a couple of days. Then, one day, an unbroken horse would have its saddlery put on and be securely tied to a tree. The herd would then set off, leaving a couple of men and the unbroken horse behind. When the herd was still just in sight – a mile or so away across the prairie – one of the cowboys would leg the other one up on to the unbroken horse. It would be so keen to return to its friends in the herd that it would be unlikely to waste too much time bucking in its anxiety to gallop off to join them and by the time it reached the herd it was usually too tired to bother. This sequence would continue until all the horses were broken and, by the time the cattle reached their destination, two jobs had been done in one!

These methods obviously make a good story but would be totally unacceptable today as they work on the basis of tiring the horse into submission rather than taking the time to understand the horse and also be understood by it. Kindness is a much better way of achieving results than forcing a horse to do things or trying to break its spirit.

Horses with very strong, dominant personalities should be treated with tact and firmness. Horses that are timid or less intelligent should be treated with sympathy and patience. Observe each individual horse carefully so that a correct assessment of its personality can be made.

The basis of successful training is the formation of trust between horse and human and this must be established from the very beginning. The sooner the foal understands and accepts what is expected of it the better, so training must start from the moment the foal is born. Regular handling and talking quietly to it will develop its confidence and it will soon realize that no harm is going to come to it. Being thoughtful and kind does not mean spoiling, however. Spoilt horses are just as unpleasant as spoilt children and in some cases they can even become dangerous.

Discipline plays a very important part in the development of any young animal. Just like children, horses are happiest when they

A young horse enjoying being loose in the paddock.

know that there are clear limits to what is right and what is wrong. There must be no deviations from the basic rules that you set out. Because horses have very little reasoning power, any reward or punishment you give must always be immediate so that the horse can relate your reaction to what it has just done. A reward or punishment must follow within seconds of the good or bad deed. A sugar lump in the collecting ring after a successful round is just as useless as a training method as chastisement with a stick if the round has not been successful – both come far too late to make sense to the horse. Praise must always be lavish and any punishment very controlled. If correction is delivered with your teeth gritted and your temper rising, many months of careful training can be wasted.

Horses have excellent memories, so your system of training must follow a logical sequence. If a problem occurs, it is then possible to revert to an earlier lesson and progress, once again, from that point. Because of the horse's excellent memory, this reversion to earlier training can still be effective even after weeks or months. As a foal, the horse must see as much of life as possible so that it does not become easily upset later when it is exposed to the outside world. Always remember that animals can react unpredictably, so do not startle or frighten the foal as it could hurt itself, or you, quite unintentionally.

The trainer must be aware of the natural reactions of the horse in the wild so that the reasons behind certain behaviour will be understood. A good trainer must possess certain qualities. First of all, he or she has to be very patient and sympathetic but also firm when the occasion arises. Above all, the trainer must have the necessary ability and knowledge to train a young horse and these are only achieved through years of observation and practice.

Time is essential for the production of the young horse, and for the production of the experienced trainer. Mistakes will be made. Provided that they are not serious, this may not be too bad a thing as we all learn through our mistakes. It is, however, the intention of this book to try to reduce the number of those mistakes.

Throughout this text, it has been assumed that the person attempting to break and train the young horse is an experienced rider and handler. Unless you have had several years' experience of dealing with youngsters and difficult, older horses, are fully competent to lunge and fit tack and completely *au fait* with correct stable management procedures, you should not attempt to train or break a young horse but should, instead, arrange to observe and assist an experienced trainer to do this work for you.

Sheila Roughton

# THE NATURAL BEHAVIOUR
# OF THE HORSE

## UNDERSTANDING THE HORSE

In order to begin to develop a sympathetic understanding of their behaviour, we must realize that horses are not humans and therefore we must try to look at life from their point of view. One of the greatest barriers to this understanding is if we try to give a horse a human personality. We must be constantly aware of the horse's natural instincts, how its nervous system works, how it thinks and the signals by which it shows its thoughts and feelings.

By nature, horses are nervous creatures but most, given quiet handling and logical training, will become docile to look after and courageous in their work. Those that remain edgy require quiet but confident handling. To obtain an insight into the natural reactions of the horse, we must first consider its development from the truly wild state.

## SURVIVAL

To survive in the wild, the horse had to develop acute senses – hearing, sight, scent, taste, touch – a strong sense of self-preservation and the ability to escape danger through flight.

### Hearing
As its ears are very movable and can be positioned at any angle, threatening or reassuring sounds can readily be detected from whichever direction they come.

### Sight
Due to the wide setting of the eyes on each side of the head, the horse has practically all-round vision. The way the ears are held or

The horse's ears will reveal its state of mind.

the expression in the eyes will reveal the horse's state of mind — calm and relaxed or worried and frightened. The eye may sometimes also reveal the mood of the horse, for example, a belligerent animal may roll its eyes, showing the whites, before attempting to kick or bite. It is worth noting at this point that this behaviour is mostly induced by misguided or inept action on the trainer's part as, left to its own devices, the horse is a gentle creature. Always treat a frightened horse with care and confidence. It will require firm but kind handling so that it does not become a danger to itself or those who deal with it.

## Scent
Horses also have an acute sense of smell which is aided by their large nostrils.

## Touch
The horse's two instinctive reactions to feeling something strange touching its back are either to buck or to rub it off. This is the natural way in which the horse's ancestors tried to remove predators from their backs.

## DEFENCE

Putting this highly efficient alarm system together with tremendous speed makes running away the most effective form of self-protection. Unless cornered, the horse's natural form of defence is always flight and it will react very quickly to anything that frightens or alarms it. If flight is not possible, the horse may resist and fight. It can kick with its hind legs, either to the side, which is called a cow kick, or straight out behind it.

While working in Iran, where packs of wild dogs were commonly encountered, I made an interesting observation. A horse being chased seldom kicked at a dog that was hanging on to its tail but preferred to rely on flight and speed to dislodge it. Had the horse momentarily stopped or slowed, one well-aimed kick would probably have killed or seriously injured the predator but, instead, flight was uppermost in the horse's mind.

The horse can also stand on its hind legs and strike out or stamp with its front legs. It can use its teeth to bite, although this form of defence is usually aimed at other horses. I was once told the horse does not know that it is vegetarian until after it has taken its first bite!

The horse also has instinctive fears that are inbred and date back to the times when its ancestors were wild. Fear of a trap explains the horse's natural dislike of a confined space with no means of escape, for example, a trailer or a dark place, jumping into a wood or over a coffin jump. Wariness of snakes causes a natural distrust of ropes or poles lying on the ground. A fear of the smell of pigs stems from the days when a wild boar, with razor-sharp tusks, could appear from the undergrowth. The scent of pigs is a long-lasting and all-pervading smell. Where transport is shared with farm stock, an unwillingness to load on the horse's part may be due to the last load carried by the lorry. Horses that habitually live in close proximity to pigs, on farms and smallholdings, quickly overcome this fear, however, as the scent is no longer associated with danger. It simply becomes part of the background of home and the security of the stable!

## SUSTENANCE

By nature, horses are nomadic, grass-eating animals living in herds that roam in search of nutritious grasses and fresh water. From a husbandry point of view, horses tend to be poor grazers as they select only the best available grass and reject coarse grasses. This practice allows coarse grazing and weeds to become predominant in a pasture. By following the correct rules of feeding, we can feed our horses to suit their very special digestive systems. Some native ponies live on a solid diet of grass and hay but most horses will require their diet to be supplemented when they are working and in winter.

Again, the fact that the domesticated native pony lives in a field with a fence around it is unnatural and certain problems can arise, such as parasites (worms) and the overeating of lush grass during times of maximum growth, such as spring and early summer, resulting in laminitis. Throughout its training the young horse must receive sufficient food to promote its healthy physical development and to give it the energy and strength to do what we ask but not so much that it becomes overexcited. Cereals can have a very alcoholic effect on horses and, therefore, may cause unnecessary problems both in their training and in their management. As with humans, the tolerance of alcohol can vary. Half a pint of beer can put some people in trouble, others can absorb many pints without showing any effects. So it is with horses. One horse will make good use of a high cereal intake, while for others a mere whiff of oats can cause endless trouble. I once successfully evented a horse, including three day events, on good quality hay alone. To feed her oats was courting disaster! I would point out, however, that she was an exception and that this should not be taken as a general rule for feeding horses in hard work. In general, oats should not be fed to ponies as they do seem to make them overexcited and difficult to handle.

In the wild, horses use their sense of smell and taste to differentiate between good and harmful types of food. Domesticated horses can be remarkably careless, however, and it is therefore important to check any horse paddock for poisonous plants, trees and hedges.

## HERD MEMBERSHIP

Horses have a strong herd instinct and do not like being alone. They are gregarious and will replace the herd with either their stable or field companions. The stable or field will thus become the place in which they feel safe and secure. This explains why they are often more reluctant to leave the yard than to return! This natural instinct can be used successfully in training as a young horse will often follow other horses happily. Horses are happiest when they are in sight of each other but can form attachments to other animals if there are no other horses nearby. If horses are to be used alone, for example, in competitions, it is wise to separate them during work and exercise. It is bad training to give them a constant companion on exercise. A bond will then develop between the two animals and it is to be expected that they will resent this bond being broken when asked to perform on their own.

This desire to stay together can cause nappiness in young horses and this problem will be dealt with later.

When several horses are turned out together, they will revert to their natural lifestyle. A pecking order will become established, with the strongest character taking the role of the leader and each horse knowing its place in the group, down to the weakest character who is last in line. If horses are turned out on their own, they may gallop around and injure themselves looking for company, so it is advisable for them to have a field companion or at least be in sight of another horse. Very valuable animals, entire colts or stallions are best put out on their own in a small, well-fenced paddock within sight of companions, as they could injure each other if turned out together. Horses are rather contrary creatures in that they hate to be alone but will then squeal and kick at each other when put together!

If several ponies are to be turned out together on a regular basis, it is advisable to remove their hind shoes. At my local branch of the Pony Club, approximately 40 strange ponies are turned out together for their week of camp. All the hind shoes are removed and, after a quick canter round the field and a couple of minor skirmishes while the pecking order is established, they all settle down into groups. It is amazing that this is possible but I think that the main criterion is a large enough field, with enough grass for everyone. Another factor is that the ponies are probably doing more work than they are used to and are therefore too tired for much squabbling!

It must not be forgotten that this natural way of life – roaming, feeding and moving on again – means that the horse is designed to have plenty of exercise and it is totally unnatural for it to be shut in a stable for many hours each day. It is very beneficial, both physically and mentally, for the horse to have some freedom in a field daily. If this is not practical, it is even more important that it receives regular exercise.

## COURAGE

A horse's natural instinct is to avoid confrontation through flight rather than to offer belligerent resistance to danger as horses are usually timid, suspicious and frightened of the unknown. An understanding trainer can build up the horse's courage but when it is frightened by something, its confidence must be restored. Genuine fear cannot be conquered by discipline because once a horse has panicked it will become insensitive to everything, including pain.

Bad behaviour is usually due to confusion, muddled training that is lacking in logical progression or incorrect handling, especially when the horse is young. As I have already mentioned, horses have excellent memories but these can work equally well against them as for them. If they are frightened by people or circumstances they will never forget the experience.

Horses are creatures of habit and need a routine so that they can feel secure and relaxed. If they become anxious about when the next feed or drink is coming or what is going to happen next, they can develop all sorts of stable vices which are not only annoying but can be detrimental to their health.

## A DESIRE TO PLEASE

Most horses want to please and take pleasure in pleasing their trainer, owner or rider. All training must be done on a reward or correction basis and the horse must always be rewarded or praised when something is done well. The voice of the trainer is of vital importance. Horses respond to the tone of the voice not the actual words spoken. They can be rewarded by a kind, encouraging tone or scolded by a sharp rebuke. Always speak to the horse kindly on your approach to it, in order not to frighten it. Then go to its shoulder and pat its neck in greeting. Remember that mistakes are generally due to human error but, if punishment is deserved, it must be given immediately, just like the reward.

## HANDLING

A horse must have confidence in its handler but must also respect him or her. The pecking order that I have already described must also be firmly established between horse and handler, so that *you* are in charge. The horse must be treated firmly and fairly so that when it does something well it is praised by your voice and given a pat. If it does not do as it is told, a scold from the voice and a quick smack on the quarters should be enough. *Never* hit a horse anywhere near the head as it may well become headshy.

Mishandling the horse can result in it becoming confused and nervous. It is vital to remember its natural instincts and remain in sympathy with its way of thinking to achieve success.

The golden rules are: speak quietly; handle gently; avoid sudden movement. Any form of aggression or attempt to force a result will probably result in failure.

# HANDLING A FOAL

If you have bred your own foal you can begin its education from day one. If you buy a weaned foal, you may have to start at the beginning if the previous owner has not done much handling. The handling of the foal should start at birth. If everything has gone well during the delivery, the foal will probably be on its feet, looking for milk, within half an hour. This is an instinctive action as, in the wild, the foal must be ready to run with the herd as soon as possible. Any weak or damaged foals would soon be caught by predators.

Some mares, especially if this is their first foal, will be a little frightened by the whole procedure and their udders may also be sore and ticklish. In these cases, the mare will need encouragement to allow the foal to suckle. She will have to be held and the foal taken to the udder. Suckling is a vital activity as it helps in the bonding process between the mare and foal. Furthermore, the colostrum (the first milk) contains important antibodies. It also aids in the process of passing the meconium, the first droppings.

If the foal has to be carried to the mare, put one arm around its quarters and the other securely around the chest. In this way, a young foal can easily be carried from one place to another. The mare and foal must not be left until the first suckling has taken place. Filly foals are normally quicker to grasp what to do than colt foals but it is vital that this first suckling is actually witnessed.

Foals tend to be born at night so their first day is generally spent in the stable. Of course, many foals are born in the field but it is easier to supervise the first crucial hours if they are in a stable. Most studs have a series of different-sized paddocks for the mares and foals, depending on their age. They will start off in a small turn-out area that has very close boarding around the fence to provide good shelter. They then proceed into larger paddocks and are gradually introduced to other mares and foals. If the foal is an only one, born at home, choose a warm day and a sheltered paddock, with high, thick hedges to provide a windbreak, for its first few days in the new and interesting world. Remember that foals, like small children, have no sense of danger, insofar as they are always drawn to the exciting and potentially harmful! Make sure that the paddock is obstacle-free and safely fenced.

Great care must be taken when turning the mare and foal out as the mare may become excited after being kept in the stable for a day or two after foaling, especially if her offspring runs ahead and leaves her. Have an experienced handler to lead the mare and various other helpers to guide the foal towards the field.

Most foals like to stay with their mothers in the beginning but then, as they grow bigger and stronger, their games will become more adventurous. Ideally, they need other foals to play with but an older horse (a nanny) will do!

The newborn foal is on its feet comparatively quickly and is soon suckling.

To start with, the mare and foal should have short periods out in the field together and spend the rest of the time relaxing in the stable. These periods will progress to all day in the field, being brought in only at night, depending on the weather. Some mares and foals may stay out at night but, generally, most Thoroughbred mares and foals come in. If they are kept out all the time, the mare must be brought in to be fed, as lactation takes a lot out of her and her diet must be supplemented to enable her to feed the foal properly. It is also important that the foal is handled every day so that it learns to enjoy human company.

When first handling a foal, crouch down to its level so that you do not look too imposing and let it get used to your voice and smell. Every morning and evening, some time must be spent getting the foal used to human attention. Rub your hands over the neck and body and down its legs and talk to it so that it becomes accustomed to your voice. This will form the basis of a good relationship between you and the foal.

## FITTING A FOAL-SLIP

A foal-slip is a mini headcollar. One of the foal's early lessons is to have its foal-slip fitted. This is usually done within the first week of its life. The longer it is left, the more difficult it becomes and therefore the more traumatic it will be for the foal. Once this is fitted, it will make handling and leading much easier. A foal-slip can be made of either webbing or leather, just like a full-sized headcollar. The same advantages and disadvantages apply: webbing is cheaper and is easy to keep clean but does not break; leather is more expensive and must be carefully looked after but is safer, as it will break if it gets caught up on something.

*Right* A foal wearing a foal-slip.

*Left* The mare and foal should be turned out in a small, well-sheltered paddock at first.

The foal-slip should be fitted in the stable while the foal is standing beside the mare. It is advisable to have a good, thick bed with deep banks around the wall to reduce the risk of injury to both foal and handler! Three people are required – one to hold the mare, one to hold the foal in the manner previously described and the third to fit the slip. Pat the foal gently all over, talk to it and, when it is fairly relaxed, put on the slip. It must fit comfortably so that the foal does not learn to associate it with discomfort or pain. It must be tight enough to prevent the foal's foot getting caught in it if it tries to scratch its head with a hind foot. It must not rub the soft, baby skin of the foal and must be checked regularly so that it does not become too tight as the foal grows. This could cause nasty sores or even scarring. Although not desirable, a correctly fitted slip can be left on while the mare and foal are out, as long as they are in an easily observed field where they can be regularly checked. Otherwise put it on to take the mare and foal to the paddock and then remove it, replacing it on the return journey to the stable.

## LEADING

Once the foal is happy about wearing the foal-slip, it should be ready to learn to be led. Two people are necessary for these lessons – the trainer and an assistant. The helper will lead the mare and the foal will naturally follow its mother. In the beginning, a piece of cloth, like a stable rubber or towel, should be placed around the base of the foal's neck. The trainer should be on the foal's left side (the nearside) and should hold the cloth in his or her left hand while the right hand is placed around its hindquarters, encouraging it to move forward. At this stage, the voice is very important and must be used to encourage and praise. Verbal commands, such as 'walk on', will be learnt at this stage and will be understood by the foal throughout its life.

The foal must *never* be pulled along. If it shows reluctance it should be pushed with the right hand and told to walk on again. If this lesson is repeated each day, the foal soon relaxes and realizes what is expected of it. It can then start to be led from the foal-slip. At first the lead rein needs to be kept quite long and with a light contact. If any difficulties are experienced, revert to putting a hand behind the hindquarters in order to encourage the foal forward.

Initially, the foal should be led behind or beside its mother but, gradually, it will learn to go in front. Once it realizes what is expected of it, it must also learn to be led from either side. This will help in its later training, when it will be expected to perform equally well to the right and left.

The foal has to learn to be led.

If the mare is easy to catch and lead, it will make these lessons easier, as the foal will often imitate its mother. The temptation of food will often overcome the reluctance of a mare to be caught and the lesson should often include catching, handling and release without stabling or treatment if this acts as a deterrent. Catching must not be associated in the horse's mind with something unpleasant, so remove from the act of catching whatever it is that the mare resents, sometimes asking no more than to catch and handle her and her foal. At other times, of course, catching will be followed by a requirement to fit in with the stable routine.

Some mares become overprotective of their foals and their behaviour becomes defensive and unreliable. Everything must be done to inspire the confidence in the mother that no harm will come to her offspring. A mare that is foal-proud in this way should be handled by the same person or people each time so that she learns to trust them.

## PICKING UP THE FEET

Another very basic lesson, which needs to be taught early on, is the handling of the foal's legs and feet. A foal will need to have its feet trimmed from the age of about six to eight weeks. To reduce the trauma of its first meeting with the farrier, the foal should be happy to allow someone to pick its legs up.

In its general handling, the foal should, by now, be used to being patted and rubbed all over. To get it to pick its feet up, run your hand down the foal's front leg while gently pushing its weight over on to the opposite leg. Pick the foot up and say 'up'. Horses learn from repeated lessons until they form a habit. It will not be long before the foal realizes what is wanted. You do not need to hold the foot for long, and neither should you raise it so high that the foal loses its balance. Do not allow the foal to snatch the foot away from you.

This lesson can be extended by picking the foot out. Not only will this help to explain to the foal that no harm is being done, it is good for the health of the feet as well.

As with leading, be very encouraging throughout the lesson and show appreciation when the foal is co-operating. Make sure that the conditions are favourable for a good result and that anything new is taught while the foal is mentally and physically able to cope. Whatever stage of training you are at, all lessons *must* end on a good note.

## TYING UP

This is another lesson that is taught in a stable containing plenty of bedding to reduce the chance of the foal slipping. The foal must learn to be tied up and left on its own but this will take time and patience. Start the lesson with the mare present.

Before this lesson begins, the foal must be confident and happy about wearing a headcollar and being led. Attach a lunge rein to the foal slip, then pass it through the tying-up ring, keeping hold of the free end.

When the foal first feels the restriction of the rein, it will probably struggle but if you do not tug but play it like a fish on a fishing line, the foal will not come to any harm. Once it begins to settle, make a big fuss of it and it will soon understand what is expected of it.

Always tie up to a piece of string tied to the ring and use a quick-release knot. The reason for this is because the foal could easily damage its neck if it pulls back on the headcollar. Because of the number of vertebrae it contains, a horse's neck is a very delicate structure and damage done while it is young could trouble the foal throughout its life.

Most horses want to please their trainers, so whenever the foal does something right, be lavish with your praise and reward so that it will want to repeat the action. The same pattern should be followed with an older horse but this might take longer as the horse will be stronger and probably more suspicious. It is always dangerous to let the horse realize its own strength.

The foal must learn to pick its feet up when asked.

## TRAVELLING

It may be necessary for the foal to learn to travel in order to acccompany the mare to stud or to a show. If the mare has foaled at home and is going to be covered again, she will need to visit the stallion seven to ten days after foaling. It is good practice for later on if the foal experiences as many unfamiliar sights and sounds as possible while in the company of its mother.

It is helpful to have your own transport so that the lesson of loading can be repeated daily and therefore becomes a common-place occurrence. Remove all the partitions, either in a trailer or a lorry, so that the mare and foal can have a large area in which to travel. A lorry is obviously preferable to a trailer because it is more stable and less noisy but lots of mares and foals travel in trailers very successfully.

Never start any lesson with a young horse on your own – always have an assistant, which usually means that three people are required to work with one mare and foal! Make the whole experience of loading as pleasant as you can. Have the ramp as flat as possible. If you are lucky enough to have a loading ramp or a small bank, this is ideal. If not, park the transport near a slope so that the angle of the ramp is reduced. Putting straw bales under the ramp will also reduce the slope but this makes for quite a big step up.

Just as when loading any horse, make sure that the vehicle is standing firmly and securely and that it is as light as possible inside the container. If using a front-unload trailer, the top half of the front ramp can be opened to let in extra light.

In the beginning, a small foal can be persuaded up the ramp in the same manner as is used when teaching it to be led. Put your right arm around the foal's hindquarters and your left arm around the chest (when standing on the nearside; vice versa when standing on the offside) and push it forward. If straw bales are used underneath the ramp, two people holding a foal in this way can lift it up on to the ramp.

Once the foal is in the transport, make a fuss of it – stroke it, speak gently and encouragingly to it and maybe give it a small feed, depending on what age it is. When it is confident about going into transport and is quite relaxed about staying in with the ramp up, take it and its mother for a short journey. They should travel loose in the box.

Horses must always be driven sympathetically and carefully and this is especially important in the beginning. Be careful at roundabouts and sharp corners, drive slowly and watch out for low-hanging trees which may make sudden and alarming noises on the roof.

A loading ramp is ideal when teaching a foal to load into a lorry or trailer.

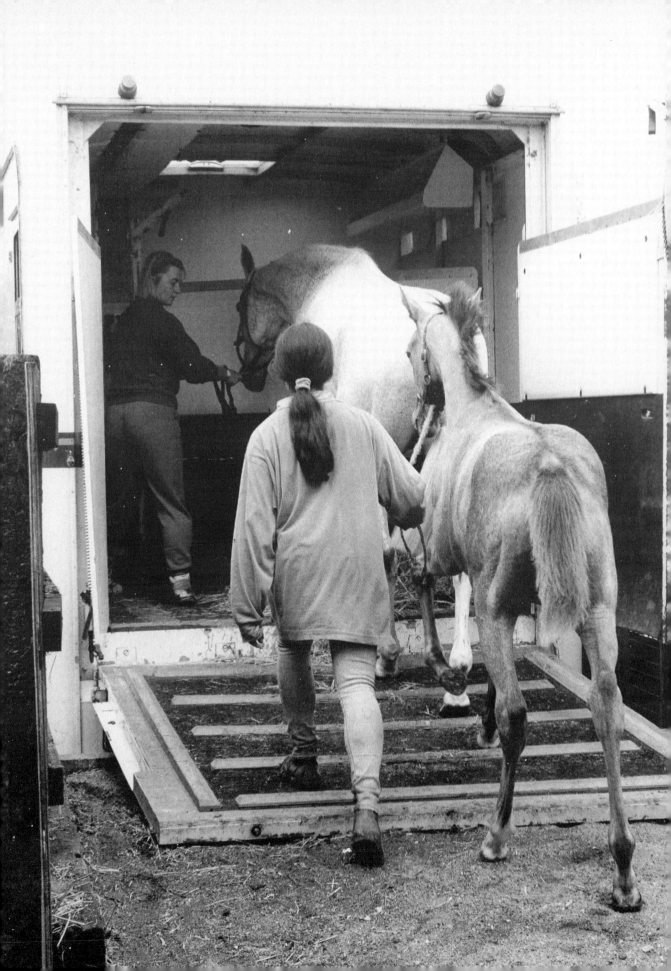

## HORSE SHOWS

Showing a mare and foal has both its good and its bad points. Obviously, if the mare and foal are successful, this will increase their value. It will also introduce the foal to the razzmatazz of the showground and everything that goes on in this new world. It also has to learn to concentrate on being led and behaving itself when there are far more exciting things to look at and be doing!

The drawbacks are that endless travelling cannot be good for young, undeveloped bones and the foal also does not have its normal amount of time for rest and play. In my experience, just a couple of shows towards the end of the season are ideal but, then, I am not obsessed by the showing game!

## CASTRATION

This can be done as soon as the testicles are down. Many owners prefer to have it done just before weaning so that the foal is still with its mother during the trauma. Others prefer to leave it until much later so that the youngster will develop more muscle. The drawback to this is that colt foals usually become very playful and although it is quite amusing for a sweet, fluffy foal to stand up and box with its front feet, it is not so funny when a big, strong two-year-old does the same! If they are left uncastrated, they must be put with colts or on their own, and have firm, authoritative handling.

## WEANING

Separation from its mother is the next major lesson in the life of the foal and should be completed by six months. If the foal is allowed to suckle after six months, it will drag the mare down in condition and possibly make her anaemic, especially if she is in foal again. Weaning can be done in several different ways:

- Separate the mare and foal and stable each out of earshot of the other;
- Have several mares and foals together in a field and gradually remove one mare at a time, until the youngsters are left on their own with a 'nanny';
- Separate the mare and foal but keep them within earshot, so that the foal knows the mare is not far away.

However the weaning process is done, the foal will need to be stabled at first and then turned out with other horses, preferably youngsters. In my experience, most foals will begin to wean themselves if they are turned out with other mares and foals or sensible 'nannies'. If the weaned foal is then turned out again with the company it already knows, the whole process becomes far less traumatic.

The mare should be turned out in a fairly bare paddock so that her milk production will be limited and she has to move around a lot to graze enough to satisfy her appetite.

The foal should have a paddock that enables it to have ample space for play, plenty of clean water, some form of safe shelter and safe fencing. The grass must be of good quality and free from worms and hazards that are likely to cause it harm.

If the mare is not in foal again, the foal can be left with its mother until the following spring, in which case both must be given sufficient concentrate feed and plenty of hay throughout the winter. By the time the foal has become a yearling, it will obviously be more independent and then weaning can be done with little or no fuss.

## THE YEARLING AND TWO-YEAR-OLD

The pattern for the next few years is now set. During the winter months, the youngster should be out by day and in at night. In bad weather, it may be necessary to keep them in all the time. If it is possible, youngsters do very well if yarded. If it becomes

Care must be taken whenever the youngster is led with a bit in its mouth.

necessary to keep them in during snowy weather, for example, they can continue to have exercise if using this system. In the summer months, they can be kept out all the time.

Throughout these couple of years, the youngster should be allowed to grow and enjoy itself. It must be fed during the winter months, to encourage proper development, and regular handling must be continued. Some youngsters will be shown in hand and this, again, has its advantages and disadvantages. One word of warning: if a youngster is shown with a bit in its mouth, it must be handled with great care. It is very easy to spoil a horse's mouth, especially when leading it. Also remember that the bones and limbs are still forming at this stage, so the body of the youngster should not be allowed to become too gross and thus put a strain on these young bones.

If it is practical to turn the youngsters out in a well-fenced paddock near a busy road or farmyard, this is an ideal way for them to become accustomed to fast or heavy traffic in a safe environment. The more that they can see at this age, in this manner, the better it will be for them when they eventually have to go out into the big, outside world.

# GENERAL STABLE MANAGEMENT
## OF YOUNG STOCK

Any domesticated animal requires looking after in order to establish confidence and a feeling of security. In the training of the young horse, the beginning of learning obedience is to stand still and move over as required. This begins during the early handling of the foal.

Routine plays a large part in the horse's wellbeing as it is very much a creature of habit. It must be able to anticipate what is going to happen so that it remains relaxed and content.

### FEEDING

As with all animals, food is required to keep the body functioning correctly and to enable the horse to perform the work asked of it. Adequate feeding prevents the horse from losing condition during adverse weather conditions and helps it to fight off disease. It also enables the horse to develop physically and generally feel good. If the young horse does not receive enough good quality food or it is given an unbalanced diet, it will never reach its full physical strength and therefore never realize its full potential.

By nature, the horse is a trickle feeder that eats for up to 16 hours a day. For this reason there is always some food in its intestines, and the total length of these is some 22 m (72 ft). To try to match this natural way of feeding, the domesticated horse must be fed little and often as it has a very small stomach. The full capacity of the stomach is about 2.7 kg (6 lb) – anything over this quantity passes through the stomach only partially digested and is therefore wasted. To keep the intestines full and to encourage healthy digestion, plenty of roughage must be fed to the stabled horse.

Many horses, especially young horses, spend their time in a grass paddock. Such pasture varies greatly in quality, depending on its geographical location, its standard of management and the time of year. Under these conditions, it may be necessary to supplement the horses' diet if they are young or working. They will always need extra food during the winter months.

To work out the correct diet for your horse, you must first assess its bodyweight. This can be done either by weighing it on a weigh bridge or by using a special tape measure bought at any good tack shop.

The horse will require 2½ per cent of its bodyweight in total food weight. Adjust the amount of concentrates to suit the work done and then add hay. A young horse that has been turned out and is growing and will later be broken will need only a small daily feed during the summer and no hay, grazing taking the place of hay. Once horses are stabled, they must have a constant supply of good hay and clean water.

The easiest method of feeding a balanced diet to a young horse is by using one of the standard compound mixes manufactured by a reputable food merchant specifically for youngsters. These companies sell cubes or mixes, made up by expert nutritionists, and suitable for the needs of every type and age group of horse. It should not be necessary to feed any additives as these will have already been added to the mix. Seek expert advice from your veterinary surgeon if an individual horse is not doing as well as it should on a particular diet.

*Below and opposite* In its natural environment the horse will eat for up to 16 hours a day.

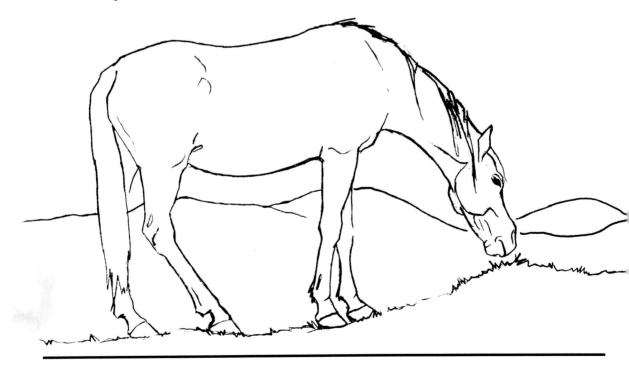

A measuring tape can be used to assess the correct weight of your horse.

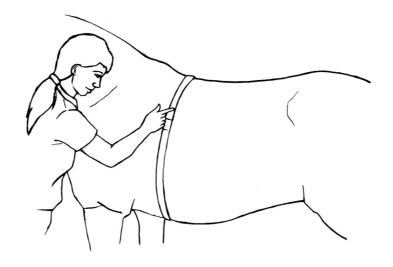

## FEET

If the horse is stabled, it is essential to keep the bedding clean, as a dirty bed can rot the feet and cause thrush. The feet should be looked after from the very beginning. The feet of a foal must not be allowed to grow out of shape as this can cause all sorts of problems in the development of its limbs, which are still growing. Regular attention will improve the shape of the foot and, if they are caught early enough, can correct certain deformities in both the limbs and feet, such as the uneven bearing of the foot on the ground,

leading to stresses in joints, twisted legs, contraction of the tendons, dishing and plaiting. With the sort of mild winters that have been experienced recently in Great Britain, coupled with most brood mares being better fed, many foals are now being born there with softer bones that can become deformed on the hard ground. The English Research Laboratories in Newmarket are now doing a terrific job of corrective shoeing in foals, which is proving both interesting and amazing in its results.

Horses should receive the attention of a farrier every four to six weeks to maintain correct balance and a level bearing surface. If the young horse has good feet, it may start its working life without shoes while it is working on a soft surface. When shoes are first fitted, lightweight racing plates are ideal as aluminium does not cause too much strain on young limbs through carrying the extra weight. I only fit front shoes at first and even this is not done until I have started the breaking-in process. The hind shoes are fitted only when the horse starts work on hard surfaces.

From the beginning it is vital that the feet are picked out daily – more often in the case of a stabled horse.

## GROOMING

Grooming is a natural social function in the wild and is performed by one horse on another in an act of friendship. For this reason, the grooming of a foal should start at a very young age. Grooming will help to form a strong bond between horse and human. If the horse nuzzles at you in return, it is usually out of closeness and friend-ship but be careful with colts, stallions and ticklish horses as a playful bite can be very painful! Grooming is necessary throughout the horse's life to keep the coat clean and the skin functioning satisfactorily and to keep it free from parasites. The skin is a gland, playing its part in cleaning the body of toxic waste. Regular grooming and the resultant massage will assist in this function. Grass-kept horses are kept fairly clean by the rain until they roll in a mud patch! The rolling patches that they use allow them to cover themselves with the communal smell of the herd. A covering of mud also helps to protect them from the weather and will discourage many parasites.

## INTERNAL PARASITES

Foals are particularly susceptible to internal parasites (better known as worms) because they have little immunity to them. They do not have worms when they are born but will soon pick them up from paddocks, especially in stud pastures that are overstocked. Horses are susceptible to different types of worm at different stages in their life. The most dangerous to the foal are ascarids and threadworms, while redworm causes the most serious worm infestations in older horses.

## Ascarids
Adult ascarids live in the small intestine and can produce up to one million eggs a day! Because of their tough, sticky, outer coat, they can survive for up to three years outside of the horse. The larvae develop inside the egg after being eaten by the foal. They hatch in the foal's gut, burrow through the gut wall and enter the blood stream. Then they migrate to the liver and the lungs and are later coughed up, then swallowed, to become egg-laying adults in the small intestine. The eggs are passed out in the droppings and the cycle starts again.

## Threadworms
These live in the small intestine and are very small. Generally, they are well tolerated and are not usually found in foals over six months old. They can cause scouring.

## Redworms
These are the most common equine parasite and a cause of major loss of performance and poor condition and may even kill. There are several different species, so named because the blood they live on colours them red. The horse loses condition due to poor absorption of nutrients from the gut. This makes its skin dry and its coat staring. As soon as larvae are eaten, they start to cause damage.

## Grass Management
Grazing must be kept clean of parasites and this can be done by cross-grazing using either cattle or sheep to reduce the amount of worm larvae, especially in the spring and autumn. Cattle feeding on coarse grass are more effective, as sheep, like horses, are close croppers, using their incisors to cut the grass rather than their tongues, as in the case of cattle. Picking up the droppings is another method but this is not always practical unless, like most of the larger studs, a dropping-picking-up machine is used. This operates on the same principle as an enormous vacuum cleaner. In small paddocks, however, a shovel, broom and wheelbarrow will probably suffice. If you harrow the paddock on a *sunny* day, this will break up the droppings and many of the worm eggs will dry out and die. The paddock can also be rested for hay, which will also break the worm cycle. Regular mucking out of paddocks will also help to maintain the quality of the grazing as it will reduce the formation of weed infestation, such as nettles and docks, in the area of horse 'lavatories'.

## Worming

Worm control is a vital part of horse management and all new horses going out into the paddocks must be wormed and kept in a stable for 72 hours first, so as not to infect the other residents. All the horses that are turned out in one field must be wormed at the same time, again so that they do not contaminate the rest.

Foals should be wormed first at six weeks and then every four to six weeks for the rest of their lives. Consult a veterinary surgeon for the safest type of wormer for very young foals. Symptoms of a heavy worm infestation are:

- anaemia;
- colic;
- little energy;
- loose droppings;
- poor condition even though eating well;
- very dry and hard skin.

This, in turn, can result in:

- stunted growth;
- internal damage that will affect the horse for the rest of its life or even kill it!

A two-year-old filly that we had to break for racing came in after the autumn sales. She was small and had a really thick, woolly coat. Although she looked all right flesh-wise, she was never right in her coat and always a little lethargic. While she was in training she never really improved and only ran once. She then returned to us for her winter holiday. We decided to have every available test and check done on her to try to improve both the way she looked and her performance. They revealed that she had redworm. She had been wormed regularly with us and again while she was in training but the vet thought that she must have been contaminated at the stud where she was born, bred and presented for the sales. The damage to her insides was so severe that she never did improve and she had to be put down as a three-year-old. Treatment from a young age is therefore *vital*.

Treatment can be given in the form of:

- powder ⎫
- granules ⎬ all of which are given in the feed;
- pellets ⎭
- paste that is given orally.

Paste is the most satisfactory method as the horse definitely receives the required dose. However cleverly the treatment is disguised in food, some horses will refuse their meal if it smells suspicious and it may put them off future feeds.

## TEETH

Care of the horse's mouth and teeth is another important aspect of stable management. Defects in the teeth can lead to many problems previously attributed to incorrect bitting. Just as injudicious feeding can affect temperament and performance, especially in dressage, so neglect of the teeth may well be a contributory cause in bitting problems. Furthermore, the best food money can buy will not benefit a horse with mouth problems.

Like a human being, a horse has two sets of teeth during its life. First of all, it has a set of milk teeth, which are small, have a definite neck and are very white. At two and a half years of age these begin to be replaced by the permanent teeth, which are much larger and yellower in colour. It is important that the teeth are checked from a very early age so that any abnormalities can be spotted and corrected before they cause a problem.

Horses have four different types of teeth:

- molars – the large teeth at the back of the mouth that are used for grinding;
- incisors – the front teeth that are used for biting food, for example, grass;
- tushes – found only in adult horses and normally only in males, although, in some cases, mares also have them. They are found between the incisors and the molars on both jaws, towards the front of the mouth;
- wolf teeth – small, extra teeth usually found in the upper jaw, close to the first molar tooth. They vary in size and root depth and are generally best removed by a veterinary surgeon or equine dentist as they can cause unnecessary problems with bitting.

The horse's mouth.

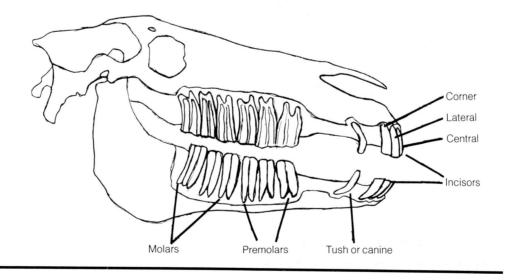

Corner
Lateral
Central

Incisors

Molars          Premolars          Tush or canine

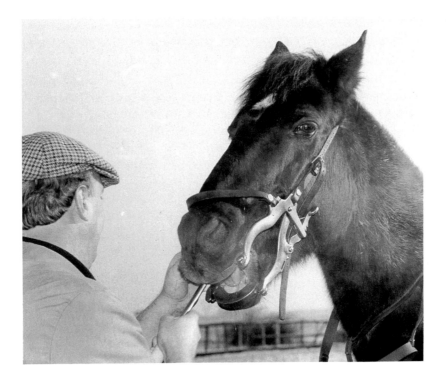

A horse's teeth being rasped. The mouth is held open with a special gag.

The main difference between human and horse teeth is that the latter continue to grow throughout the horse's life. It is generally believed that the horse feels no pain when work is done on its teeth because they lack the nerves that are found in human teeth.

Due to the grinding action of the teeth and the fact that the upper jaw is wider than the lower, the molars need regular rasping. If they are left unattended, they become sharp. These sharp teeth cause the inside of the cheeks and the tongue to become lacerated, which makes it uncomfortable for the horse to eat so that food is either left or dropped out of the mouth while the horse is eating (quidding). These wounds also cause pain while the horse is being ridden, which can give rise to unnecessary arguments between horse and rider.

To avoid such problems, the teeth need rasping by your veterinary surgeon every six months at least and in some cases more regularly. A special gag should be used to ensure that the job is done safely. Young or old horses need special attention. If a tooth is missing in one jaw, the corresponding tooth in the other jaw will keep growing up or down into the gap, making it impossible for the horse to eat properly. The whole digestive process can become less efficient as a result.

A horse's teeth do not often develop cavities as ours do. They can become decayed but their thick enamel coating acts as a very good protection.

# THE EQUIPMENT REQUIRED FOR BREAKING

## AN EXPERIENCED TRAINER

The process of breaking requires unlimited amounts of patience, sensitivity and understanding from anyone who embarks upon it. Because of the many types of horse – all of whom have individual temperaments and past experiences which make them behave and react differently – it is necessary to have a wealth of experience in all fields of equestrianism on which to draw. It is also *vital* to have an experienced helper. In my case, I had an excellent young man who was totally unflappable and whom I knew would never let go of the horse at a crucial moment.

It is essential that confidence is built up between the rider and the assistant as any nervousness between them will immediately be sensed by the horse and will frighten it. Some trainers prefer to stay on the ground so that the horse hears their voice coming from the same place throughout but in my experience it does not appear to make much difference. The important thing is that if your assistant is to help from ground level, they must be obviously relaxed and laid back but very quick to react if necessary. If they are to be the rider, they must be a good rider, have good balance, be brave and not get bucked off as this will frighten the horse. As I get older, the role of the trainer on the end of the lunge line is becoming increasingly more attractive than getting on the horse!

## SAFETY

It must be remembered that a certain element of risk is involved in breaking horses because, if they do not understand what is happening or become frightened, they can behave unpredictably. To reduce the risks, certain rules have to be observed.

First of all, the person who is going to mount *must* wear the correct dress. It is vital that a crash helmet (in the UK British Standard BS4472) is worn to protect the head. (In the UK, the BSI is currently revising its safety standard, so the number may change to BS6473.) No loose clothing should be worn but a body protector is essential to prevent bruising in the event of a fall. Riding boots and gloves should be worn. The person who remains on the ground, holding the lunge rein, must also be sensibly dressed: no loose clothing, which may distract or frighten the horse, sensible shoes or boots, a hard hat and, above all, gloves.

I also think it is advisable to have personal accident insurance when riding, and especially breaking, horses. Riding is considered a high-risk sport and accidents do happen. All precautions must be taken to reduce the risk of injury but it is too late to wish that you had taken out cover after the accident has happened. Luckily, I never made a claim on my own insurance as a result of breaking horses but I did from my evening exploits!

Before the breaking of a horse can begin, it is important to know the history of the particular animal. If it is your own horse, this is comparatively easy as you will know exactly how much handling it has had and how it reacted to various new experiences. Tackling

Always be careful and leave plenty of room when introducing the horse to new equipment.

other people's horses is not quite so easy. The horses that are a problem are the ones that have begun to be broken, have come up against a particular problem and have become frightened. In some cases, the owner will be embarrassed, so will not admit to having had any trouble and just leave you to find out. Luckily, I did not have too many of these.

Generally speaking, if the horse has been well handled and is confident and the breaking procedure proceeds at a pace set by the horse, things will go smoothly.

Be very careful when introducing new equipment to the horse, in order not to frighten it. Always give the horse and yourself plenty of space when first attaching equipment, so that if the horse moves quickly no one will be trapped. It is also vital that, when the horse is mounted for the first time, this is done in an indoor school or paddock *never* in a stable.

Monty Roberts, an American, has visited Britain in order to demonstrate how to break horses in an exceptionally fast time. He obviously has a peculiar talent and uses a brilliant rider. He works on the theory of communication with the loose horse – allowing it to make the first move towards meeting the human. He uses a large pen of about 20 m (66 ft) in diameter and, after the preliminaries are completed, he puts his rider up. It works very well for him but it must be remembered that he and his rider are experts and I would not advise the use of this type of pen by the majority of private or commercial breakers.

## FACILITIES

A safe environment and an experienced trainer are more important than the actual facilities. Nowadays, however, it is relatively easy to hire facilities, such as an indoor school. In fact, if using an indoor school involves the horse being loaded into some form of transport and travelled a short distance, the horse is receiving twice the amount of education!

It is important to have use of an indoor school, outdoor arena or small paddock so that you have an enclosed area with sufficient space. At all times you must have an assistant in whom you have absolute confidence. Later, when the time comes to mount the horse, an additional helper will be required to leg the rider up.

## EQUIPMENT

All the equipment used must be well fitting and in good repair although it need not be in the first flush of youth. Young horses have a tendency to chew and/or rub the equipment used because, in the beginning, it will feel strange and probably rather itchy.

## Boots

The horse will require brushing boots on each leg. These are worn for protection as, during the first part of breaking, which is lungeing, the horse will be very unbalanced and runs the risk of knocking its legs with its own feet. This can cause discomfort and, in more serious cases, scarring. The most effective boots I have found are made of padded material with Velcro fastenings. They are very soft and do not cause chaffing of the soft, baby skin. Velcro fastenings are also quick and easy to secure and remove, so the time one spends in the vulnerable position of crouching down around the horse's legs is reduced. Accustom the horse to the sound of Velcro before you attempt to put these boots on. Over-reach boots may also be needed on the front feet if the going is deep.

## Roller and Breastplate

A roller and breastplate will be needed to accustom the horse to having something tightened around its girth area. A properly designed breaking roller can be purchased but it is not absolutely necessary. It is essential, however, that the roller used has a breastplate attached to it to prevent it slipping back and acting as a 'bucking strap'. The roller can be made of any number of different types of material but, whatever it is made of, it must be soft so that it does not chafe behind the horse's elbows. I use a full-sized numnah underneath the roller, which acts as padding and also gets the horse used to having something on its back. Leather rollers must be cared for in the same way as other saddlery, with regular cleaning and softening. All too often, breaking rollers that are used infrequently are left to one side in the tack room and become hard and brittle, making them a cause of discomfort to the horse and a threat to the safety of the trainer.

## Saddle and Bridle

An old saddle and bridle will also be required. They must be in good repair and must fit the horse but should not be too valuable. The saddle will require a soft girth, stirrup leathers and irons and the aforementioned numnah. It is also comforting for the rider to have either a neckstrap or a holding strap fixed on to the front arch of the saddle. It is sensible to keep a couple of fingers tucked into this so that, if the youngster moves quickly and unexpectedly, the horse's mouth does not receive a tug or jab.

## Bit

The bit used for breaking is a matter of choice. I prefer a rubber-covered lightweight, jointed snaffle as this is softer for delicate mouths unused to a bit and the horse will be comfortable from the

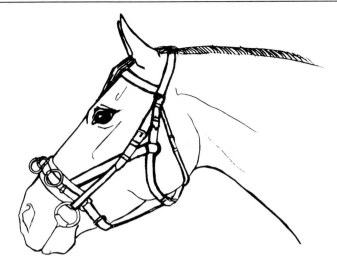

A properly fitted cavesson.

beginning. A mouthing bit can be used. This has keys on the mouth-piece, which are intended to encourage the horse to champ on the bit and create saliva, so keeping the mouth wet and responsive. My experience of this is that the horse never really forgets playing with the keys and, for years to come, continues to play with the bit. This can become an infuriating habit. Throughout training, I believe that one should start the way one means to carry on, which means that there should be no unsteadiness in the mouth and saliva should be produced by acceptance of the bit, not by champing.

### Lungeing Cavesson and Rein

A cavesson headcollar and lunge rein will be required for lungeing. The cavesson is a large, padded headcollar which is put on over the top of the bridle and has three rings attached to the front and sides of the noseband. The lunge rein is made of webbing and should be about 9 m (30 ft) long. The rein is secured to the centre ring of the cavesson so that the horse can go clockwise or anti-clockwise around the trainer while being lunged. The headcollar must be cleaned regularly and kept supple, as should the leather parts of the lunge rein. These items are often neglected, leading to the discomfort of the horse or the breaking of the lunge rein because the leather has become brittle.

If you are not able to use a lungeing cavesson, the lunge rein can be attached in several different ways. It can be clipped to the outside cheekpiece of an ordinary cavesson noseband and then brought round the nose and threaded through the ring of the snaffle bit so that it does not pull the bit through the horse's mouth; a spur strap can be attached to both snaffle rings under the chin and the rein then clipped on to the strap; or the lunge rein can be threaded through the inside ring, over the top of the head and attached to the opposite bit ring. This method is more severe than the others.

## Lunge Whip

Another necessity is a long whip, which is used in conjunction with the voice to control the horse. It is seldom, if ever, used on the horse. These vary in their length and weight, so one must be chosen to suit the individual breaker.

## Dressage or Schooling Whip

This is a long stick that is an essential piece of equipment, although it will not be required until the horse is mounted. Used properly, with a flick from the rider's wrist, this whip will just touch the horse's side behind the rider's leg to reinforce the leg aids.

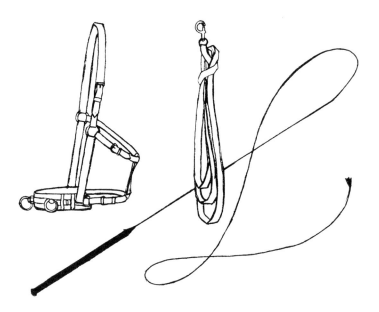

Lungeing cavesson, rein and whip.

## Side-reins

These are a pair of adjustable reins (preferably made of leather because the webbing ones tend to slip), with spring clips. They come in several different designs, such as doughnut ones, which have a large rubber ring in them about 15 cm (6 in) from the end, ones with an elastic insert positioned in a similar place, or just plain leather straps. I prefer the latter as I believe that both the doughnut and the elastic insertions encourage the horse to lean on the rider's hand. Side-reins are used as a substitute for the rider's hand and they should encourage the horse to seek and take the bit with confidence. If the horse becomes accustomed to just taking more and more, it will then try to lean on the rider's hand while being ridden.

In the beginning, side-reins are used to introduce the horse to the contact offered by the rider's hand and, later, to help to improve the horse's way of going. At first side-reins are fitted quite

Necessary equipment for beginning to break-in a horse. *Left to right* Breaking roller, brushing boots, side reins, cavesson headcollar, snaffle bridle, lunge rein.

loosely in order not to restrict the horse's movement and thereby causing it to become frightened or to panic. At the beginning of any lungeing session, with a horse of any age, always warm the horse's muscles up before attaching the side-reins.

The side-reins should be fitted to be just in contact with the mouth, as, if they are too short, they cause the back muscles to tighten instead of encouraging the horse to relax its back and be loose. If the horse has a neck that is set on too low, you can use a German-designed strap, with a piece of elastic inserted into it, which attaches between the bit and the girth. This prevents the horse from raising the underside of its neck in transitions and therefore developing the wrong muscles.

The alternative to side-reins is to use webbing running reins, which are attached to the girth and pass up through the bit rings then back to the saddle. This enables the horse to carry its head at whatever height it finds comfortable but ensures that it does not poke its nose out too far in front of its body which would allow the hocks to trail out behind it and the horse's weight to fall on to its forehand.

## Long Driving Reins

Long-reins are also made from webbing and should be about 7.6 m (25 ft) long. They are not used by everyone who breaks horses in and should only be used by an experienced trainer. The trainer must also be very fit!

# BREAKING-IN

'Breaking-in' is the traditional description of the basic training, lungeing and mounting of the horse for the first time. It is a totally inadequate term as it gives entirely the wrong impression of what really happens. It conjures up a picture of people taking an untouched, wild creature from a field, putting on all its saddlery and then a rider leaping in its back, resulting in the terrified horse bucking and fighting to rid itself of such an unpleasant experience. The general public are often influenced by Wild West sagas of the cinema and on television, showing bucking broncos, whooping cowboys and evidence of brute force. Although this may once have taken place in the Wild West, it is far removed from the process employed by humane horse breakers in the western world.

A more accurate description would be along the lines of 'gentling' the horse, as the Americans say. If the horse has been handled and educated correctly from the beginning, the breaking or 'backing' part is purely a continuation of this training. The basic principles of communication and co-operation have already been laid down and the horse will already know how to respect and obey its trainer. A bond based on trust will have been formed and the horse will know that obedience brings reward.

Some horses prove more difficult in the early stages of training, very often because they have been neglected or mishandled as foals and/or youngsters. Others may prove difficult for reasons of temperament, for example, a sharp quick-thinking horse, often a potential star, or a nervous horse who lacks confidence in both its handler and its surroundings.

Some years ago, when I was working in a well-known show-jumping yard, we used to receive a regular supply of young, unbroken horses from Ireland. In one particular shipment there

Two-year-olds returning from a training gallop.

was an extremely nervous four-year-old bay gelding with a burn mark around his neck. He was untouchable, purely because he was terrified. He was beautifully made, with impeccable breeding for jumping, but had to be herded out of the lorry and into a barn as we could not get near him. He had only been caught once in his life – to be castrated – and had otherwise been left out on the hills. He had then been lassoed to be caught for transportation to England, hence the burn mark on his neck.

Obviously this horse needed time to recover from the trauma of the journey before any form of bond could be established between him and what he considered to be terrifying humans. After hours of talking to him and just being with him, without any attempt at touching him, his curiosity got the better of him! One day, he made the first move by touching me and the first major hurdle had been overcome. From that point, steady progress was made but he always remained rather nervous and sharp in his reactions. He turned out to be a fantastic performer, starring in the Junior Three Day Event British team for three years before going on into Young Rider classes.

All training must follow a logical, progressive sequence but in a case such as this it is even more important. As I have already said, horses have incredibly long memories and this particular horse never really forgot his wild upbringing and unpleasant early experiences with humans, so he was easily confused and frightened. If anything worrying occurred, he resorted to bucking, an art he perfected! We then had to go back a step in his training and solve the problem.

The direct opposite to this horse was one that we bred at home out of an old, Thoroughbred, point-to-point mare. This filly was always very independent and caused her mother endless anxiety by always preferring to go off and play with everyone else. She was brought into a stable every night and well handled as I had students at the time and they loved playing with her. During the day she and her mother and a couple of other, resting racehorses were turned out in the paddock next to where we worked the other horses. Inbetween eating, sleeping and playing with the other horses and our lurcher dog, she used to watch. When we came to break her she was so happy and confident with us that she appeared to say, 'I've been watching what you do and it's easy!' She appeared to take everything in her stride and was never any problem.

Another problem can appear in a foal, that, through some misfortune, has been hand-reared. In their way, they can be just as difficult as the first horse I mentioned. As foals, it is very easy to spoil them so that they become overconfident and do not even receive natural discipline from their mothers. They lose respect for humans as it does not take them long to realize that they are stronger and do not have to do as they are told. This type of horse is not easy to train and, in many cases, is not worth the time, patience and money involved.

### The Three-year-old

The breaking-in process usually starts when the horse or pony is three years old. Obviously there are some exceptions to this, especially in the sphere of racing where Thoroughbreds start their careers as two-year-olds and can be entered in the Classics as three-year-olds.

Nowadays, when everyone lives their lives at tremendous speed and money has to be made quickly from young horses, some are broken and offered for sale as 'potential . . .' at three years old. Rushed early training always shows at a later date, however, when problems are bound to occur and the horse has no logical training structure to fall back on. There must also be a chance for the horse's young bones and joints to develop without too much strain. In addition, youngsters must be given time for their minds to mature – an older horse will take the stress of training far more easily than a baby.

The aim of basic training is to give the horse a systematic, logical foundation to build on for specialized work in the future. Not every horse will be a top performer but we can train each one to perform to the best of its ability. A thorough, all-round education will turn it into a much more enjoyable horse, whether it is going to be a family pet or a competition horse, while proper development of its muscles and balance will improve the chance of it staying sound much longer. What the specialized racing fraternity choose to do with their young horses is their decision but, for the trainer of horses or ponies outside the racing world, it is better to delay hard work until bones have become set and tendons strengthened, which means delaying the process until they are three to four years old.

By the time it reaches its third year, the young horse should be easy to handle in and out of the stable. It should be used to wearing a headcollar and to being led from either side. It should also tie up, pick its feet up and have confidence in, and respect for, its trainer.

I prefer to start the breaking-in of an ordinary riding horse during the summer months. This means that the youngsters can spend a large amount of each day out in the field so that they have sufficient exercise. Nowadays, horses suffer more from insufficient exercise than too much. I like to keep them in the stable overnight so that they still have the discipline of good stable manners and the familiarity of being groomed each day. This helps to form a bond between the trainer and the horse.

In some cases, such as the breaking of Thoroughbred race-horses, this has to be done during the winter so that they can go into training as two-year-olds in the early spring. These young horses are bred to mature early and are fed from a very young age, so their development is somewhat forced. They have to be stabled all the time as most of them have been living under special heat lamps to produce them for the sales. They need regular exercise each day and will also benefit from some freedom each day if this is practical. This can be given by turning them loose in an indoor, or safe outdoor, arena or a small paddock. At this age they get tired quite quickly and do not need long periods of work but they do need some exercise.

If the horse is not used to wearing brushing boots, this should be its first lesson. It must be happy to stand in its stable with its boots on before asking it to work in them. At this stage it can be led, in hand, for up to half an hour around a field, farm or even a quiet lane. This will help to prepare the horse for the physical effort required when it is put on the lunge.

## LUNGEING

After about a week, lungeing may begin but this should *only* be done by an experienced person. It is difficult to educate a horse on the lunge, so practice must have been gained by lungeing an experienced, older horse that is willing and co-operative.

Horses learn by habit, so all lessons must be given in a logical sequence and repeated until the horse is familiar with them. In lungeing, the horse is taught to respond to the trainer's voice, the whip and the aids given through the rein, so that the horse describes a circle around the trainer, maintaining a light contact with the lungeing rein. All work must be done equally on each rein so that balance is maintained through movement in each direction. At first, five minutes on each rein will be sufficient.

Throughout this training, it is important that all commands are given in a calm but firm voice, backed up by positive actions. If it thinks that its trainer is confident, the horse will gain confidence. I maintain that *any* decision is better than *no* decision, as indecisiveness has no part in the training of animals.

All domestic animals respond to the tone of the human voice not its actual words, so it is important to use the tone correctly. If a faster pace is required, the voice is used higher and more positively, going from a lower tone to a higher one, as in 'Trr–rot'. When slowing the horse down, use a softer, lower tone, going from a higher pitch to a lower one, as in 'w–a–l–k'. I usually start

A young horse working happily on the lunge.

*Opposite* In the beginning, two people are required to teach the horse how to lunge.

*Below* The trainer should form the apex of a triangle created by the lunge rein, lunge whip and horse.

my commands with 'and', the upward transitions being short and sharp: 'and trr–rot'; the downward ones slower and softer, 'a–n–d w–a–l–k'.

The circle used for lungeing must be as large as possible. If the horse is lazy and knows that it can slow down on a large circle, shorten the lunge rein and walk a small circle in the centre of the horse's circle. This will enable you to keep it working forwards. A small circle will put too much strain on a young horse, especially on its hocks, and can, in some cases, ruin its paces.

When asking a horse to halt on the lunge, always do so alongside a wall and then walk towards the horse. Never allow it to learn that it can turn in, as it will then do so when you do not want it to.

Always remember the horse is a timid animal, so you should therefore never get in front of it unless you want to stop it. If its route of escape is blocked, it will stop, so always keep yourself level with its hip while lungeing so that it is encouraged to go forward.

## Early Lungeing

Before lungeing can begin, the young horse must be quite used to being led from either side. The first lesson in lungeing will require the trainer and a helper and must be carried out where the horse will be least distracted. This, of course, is best done in an indoor school but if this is not practical then an area must be fenced in so that there are some walls that the horse will not try to jump. A temporary arrangement can be made with show jumps.

To begin with, the horse should have boots on all four legs, possibly also overreach boots and be wearing a cavesson headcollar. Using this ensures that the aids are given to the horse via its nose and not to its more sensitive mouth. The throatlash should be tightened just underneath the jawbone and the noseband tightened just underneath the cheekbone. This will prevent the cheekpieces from slipping round and rubbing or interfering with the eyes. The lunge rein is attached to the centre ring.

The trainer must be correctly dressed as described on p.38 and must be wearing gloves. The helper must be similarly dressed.

The trainer will lead the horse round on the lunge rein with the helper on the inside, behind the lunge rein. After a few circles the trainer will slowly begin to release the lunge rein and stay in the centre of the circle. He or she must stay moderately still and turn with the horse. The handler, on the inside, will let go of the horse at times but will continue to walk with the horse until it begins to understand what is expected of it. The circle should be approximately 20 m (66 ft) in diameter, with the trainer at the area of a triangle formed by the lunge rein, lunge whip and horse. The trainer will continue to use the vocal commands that have been taught while leading the horse in hand.

When the whip is first introduced, it is a good idea to stroke the horse all over its body with it while it is standing still. Always talk in a soothing tone of voice and pat the horse so that it is not frightened. The whip will be used to back up the commands given by the voice but it must never be used in a manner that will upset the horse and break the trust that has been built up between the horse and the trainer. The first lesson will probably only involve a little walking and learning to halt and walk on again. When this has been achieved on each rein, congratulate the horse by stroking it and using a 'pleased' voice. Do not get into the habit of giving titbits at random as this only encourages horses to nip or to turn in on every occasion that they are asked to halt.

If the first lungeing session has been successful and the horse is not upset by the work, the roller and breastgirth can then be fitted. It is preferable to do this while still in the enclosed arena as you will then have more room than if this is done in the stable. Of course, an indoor school is ideal because when the roller and breastgirth have been gently put on and the roller eased up into contact so that it will not slip – *not* tight – the horse can be let loose. In my experience, if they have a good buck at this stage they usually settle down quicker.

Stroke the horse all over with the whip so that it is not frightened by the whip.

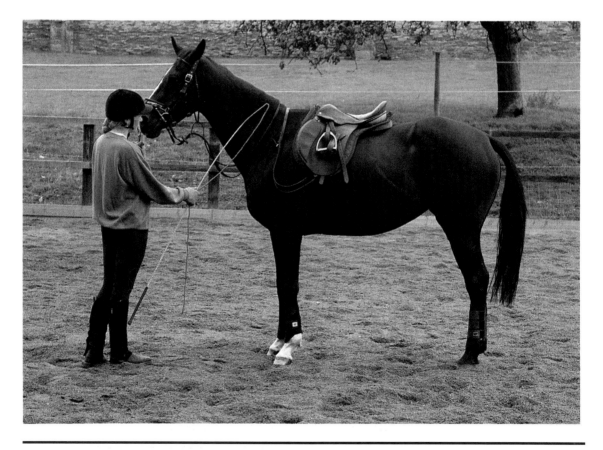

This lesson can be taught earlier, of course, and if you have handled your own youngster since birth, it will probably already be used to something being done up around its girth area. Once the roller has been fitted with a breastgirth, it can safely be left on the horse in the stable so that it can become used to it.

Lungeing must be carried out each day but only for short periods because the young horse will be unfit and unnecessary strain must not be put on its joints, especially the hocks. In the beginning, all that should be asked is for the horse to walk and trot on either rein in response to the commands given by the trainer. The progressive steps of the training should only be taken as and when the horse is ready, so I shall not say exactly when you should to move on to the next stage as this always depends on the individual horse.

### Fitting the Bit

The next target is to get a bit into the horse's mouth. This can be done either by fixing it to the cavesson headcollar or by just using the headpiece and cheekpieces of a bridle with the bit. If you use a skeleton bridle, the headpiece of the bridle lies under the head-piece of the cavesson but the cheekpieces of the cavesson thread *under* the cheekpieces of the bridle. This makes it lie flatter and is therefore more comfortable for the horse. I like to use a jointed rubber snaffle for the comfort of the horse. A straight bar rubber snaffle can encourage a horse to roll its tongue back and flip it up over the bit. This is a very annoying habit and one that is extremely difficult to correct.

### Fitting Side-reins

Once the horse has the roller fitted, I attach the side-reins, fairly loosely, to the rings on each side of the cavesson. This encourages the horse to work more correctly and gives the trainer more control. When the horse has become accustomed to the feel of the bit, the side-reins are then attached to the bit – again loosely. In no way should side reins be confused with bearing reins. Bearing reins fix the horse's head carriage to conform with the trainer's ultimate objective by using a short cut. They cause deadening of the sensitivity of the mouth, constriction of the neck and back muscles and encourage the horse to lean on the bit. Side-reins, properly adjusted, play no part in the horse carrying itself correctly and are merely there to guard against excessive movement of the head and neck, such as the lowering of the neck below the point of true control or, conversely, tossing or raising of the head above the point of control. They must never be done up so that the horse feels restricted and therefore panics. Nor should they encourage the horse to lean on them.

### Fitting the Saddle

Once the horse is lungeing quietly in the roller, it will be ready for the saddle. Always use a numnah under the saddle so that it is warm and comfortable on the horse's back. Getting the horse confident and comfortable in its boots, saddle and bridle and going quietly on the lunge will take anywhere from three days to a month, the average being about a week. It is very imporant that the horse is confident in its trainer and familiar with the equipment and its surroundings. It is also vital that this first stage of training is carried out quietly, calmly and methodically.

When the saddle has been introduced, the stirrups should be tied up at first so that nothing is moving and frightening the horse. Once it has got used to the saddle with the stirrups tied up, they can be let down so that they do flap against its sides and it can learn not to be apprehensive about them. Before moving on to the stage of backing, it is also important that the horse becomes accustomed to someone standing above it and touching it all over. At the end of a lungeing session, patting and talking to the horse, including patting the saddle and hindquarters, will be of benefit. This can continue while grooming and using a box or stool to stand on gets the horse used to having someone above it.

There are differing opinions about the amount of time that should be spent on a youngster before it is backed. Some people spend a month or more, so that the horse becomes very obedient to the voice and relatively supple and fit but for many this can be a disadvantage! I consider lungeing to be very important throughout a horse's training but I prefer to lunge the horse for only as long as it takes for it to become obedient to my commands and used to the equipment before I mount. For some time after the initial mounting, lungeing continues each day before I get on.

## BACKING

It is preferable to back a horse in a quiet, enclosed space and for this I always use an indoor school. Unexpected outside disturbances at a critical moment are far less likely to occur here and therefore the horse, trainer and rider will all be more relaxed. The enclosed space should not be too confined. A large loose box might be tempting but could be the source of potential danger. Some trainers use a stable for the initial backing but I consider this to be dangerous as, if the horse does become frightened and panic, there is no room for manoeuvre and the situation will only worsen. When deciding on the suitability of an enclosed area for backing, not only must the floor space be considered but also the headroom. A low roof or beams could cause accidents should the horse react violently when first backed.

Provided the preparation and the run-up to backing have been done quietly and progressively, a horse should not unduly resent the loss of its absolute freedom to please itself. However, at some stage in training the horse will probably show resentment and confrontation will ensue when the will of the horse clashes with the will of the trainer. It is preferable that this confrontation takes place early in the training when the horse is less physically developed, than later, when it is stronger and more mature. This clash of wills must be won by the trainer or the horse will, at best, become rebellious and, at worst, unmanageable in later life.

Three people are required for backing: the trainer to hold the horse's head, the rider and someone capable of giving the rider a good leg-up. The rider should be fairly lightweight but it is more important to be competent, calm and brave, as nervousness on the part of the rider will be transmitted to the horse and it, too, will become nervous and tense. If you are backing a pony, it is essential to use a small, very light, experienced adult – never a tall or heavy adult or a child.

Lungeing should continue. The horse should be lunged thoroughly on each rein wearing boots, saddle, bridle and with the side-reins just in contact. Added to this basic equipment should be

To begin with, the rider just leans across the horse's back.

a neck strap for the rider to hold should the horse buck. The neck strap should be loosely attached to the front Ds of the saddle so that it does not slip down out of the rider's reach if the horse lowers its head and neck in preparation to buck or take some other evasive action. Before the mounting lesson begins, the horse should have any extra energy used up and be relatively tired through having been lunged.

With some horses, it may be necessary for the first backing lesson to be restricted to the rider being legged up and down, from both sides, and just lying across the horse. During this process, the rider should pat and stroke the horse, accompanied by soothing and encouraging words from the trainer to reduce the horse's nervous reaction to such a strange experience. Next, the horse should be led forwards, with the rider still lying across its back, just a few steps at a time. Generally, horses do not object to the weight on their back but problems can occur when they are asked to move carrying the unexpected burden! No attempt to put the right leg over the horse's back and sit up must be made until the horse is quiet and happy with the weight of the rider. If the horse should become frightened when it moves forward carrying the weight for the first time, the rider is in a good position to slide off safely and start again.

Once the horse can be led confidently around the training area with the rider lying over the saddle, it can be halted. The rider slips off and is now legged up again, keeping the upper body low to the horse's neck, and slowly puts their right leg over the horse's back, being careful not to touch it. Once again, the trainer leads the horse forward in walk and talks encouragingly to it and then the rider will sit up slowly. It is important at this stage that the trainer talks to the horse, rather than the rider, as a bond of confidence must be established between the horse and the trainer. At a later stage, the rider can take over this responsibility. If all goes well, the horse can be put back out on to a large circle around the trainer, who remains in control. Before trotting, the rider should 'rise' in walk a few times so that the horse will not become alarmed when the rider starts to go up and down as it begins to trot. At this stage, the rider must be careful to return to the saddle lightly, as a heavy contact on the horse's back might startle it.

Very gradually, the rider should start to take over the control of the horse by using clear voice aids alongside gentle leg and rein aids. Aim to have the horse walking and trotting quite confidently on the lunge, moving forward from the legs and slowing down from the hand and voice. Initially, voice control should precede hand control. As the horse becomes more used to the aids, so the voice should become a secondary aid and the rein control should become predominant. If all has gone smoothly, the horse is now ready to be let off the lunge. Training should continue in the enclosed area and the pupil will benefit from having an older horse to follow in the early stages.

If the horse displays no concern or resentment when it is first leant on, backed and lunged, it will be possible to ride loose very quickly. On the other hand, if there is any anxiety or disobedience, it is best to proceed more slowly.

## LONG-REINING

Long-reining is a considerable art and one that is practised by few trainers these days. It should *never* be attempted by the inexperienced. The aim is to have as light a contact on the reins as possible, working the horse forward and encouraging it to take a contact. There must never be any backwards movement of the

Long reining using a bridle and roller.

trainer's hand. It must never be forgotten that tremendous leverage can be exerted on the horse's mouth by 7.6 m (25 ft) of rein, especially in the later stages when this rein is passed through the stirrup iron. Any roughness on the trainer's part, or sudden or unanticipated movement on the horse's part, may cause a great setback in the training of the pupil, not to mention physical injury to the bars of the mouth and corners of the lips. For this reason, long-reining should be practised by experienced trainers only and is not recommended as a general stage in breaking by those who are less capable.

To long-rein the horse, the equipment needed is a bridle, cavesson, roller, side-reins and long-reins. One long-rein is fitted to the nearside ring of the cavesson and the other rein is fitted to the outside ring and then threaded back through the centre terret, or ring, on the roller. To introduce the horse gently to wearing two reins, lunge in the normal way, allowing the outside rein just to lie loosely over the horse's back. Proceed carefully in walk on each rein. It may take several sessions for the horse to accept the second rein in trot in each direction, with the rein either over the horse's back or around its hindquarters. Before proceeding any further, the horse must be fully confident and calm. Just like lungeing, this lesson must be taught in a quiet, enclosed place so that the risk of the trainer losing either rein, and thus frightening the horse, is minimized. Once the horse has fully accepted both reins, attach them direcly to the bit, threading them through the side terrets and back to the trainer's hands.

The closer the trainer can be to the horse, the better the control but the contact on the rein *must* be sympathetic and allowing, following the same principles as for correct equitation.

The advantages of long-reining are that the horse can be worked on straight lines and circles and make transitions. In a *quiet* rural environment, it can also be taken down lanes and introduced to the big outside world from an early stage in its training. If this is done, an assistant must always go with you and remain at the horse's head in case it becomes frightened. As this modern world we live in becomes more highly mechanized and everyone and everything moves faster, long-reining on any road is becoming increasingly dangerous and is therefore mostly impractical and inadvisable.

The disadvantages of long-reining fall into two main categories:

- the trainer may lack the expertise to maintain proper control with two reins;
- the trainer may lack the required fitness to keep up with the horse and therefore 'hangs' on the reins, giving entirely the wrong feeling in the contact for the horse.

Horses that have been subjected to faulty long-reining in their training will very often reveal the fact in later life. Their paces tend to become short and stilted and their head-carriage is often overbent. It is therefore often more beneficial to lunge the horse with one rein and do a competent job than to run the risk of a disaster on two.

## FURTHER EARLY TRAINING

Even though the youngster has now been backed and is ridden off the lunge, work on the lunge should continue in order to improve obedience and balance. The trainer must make sure that he or she can keep the horse working forward, using the lunge whip and the voice, in order to accustom it to the leg aids, and the rein to transmit the rein aids. At this stage all lungeing work is done at walk and trot. In the beginning, with an unbroken three-year-old, no training session should exceed 15 minutes on the lunge. As the horse becomes stronger and fitter, these sessions can be lengthened, although, if the horse is to be ridden as well, the whole session should still not exceed half to three-quarters of an hour. As soon as the horse shows any sign of being tired, it must be given a break on a loose rein if being ridden or without side-reins if on the lunge, so that it can stretch downwards and forwards with its neck.

In the early stages of breaking, the young horse need not be ridden each day. The muscles along its back will become stiff when it is first asked to use them so it may be advantageous to lunge it on alternate days only. Another way of exercising a youngster in an interesting, but also educational, way is to loose-school.

## LOOSE-SCHOOLING

For this, it is essential to have an indoor school that is not too large or a high, boarded, outdoor arena. The horse is saddled as for work, with boots on all four legs and possibly overreach boots also. A bridle without reins and an old saddle with a numnah underneath will be needed.

The school must be empty except for a cone or a jump wing in each corner for the horse to go round. If the school is small enough, the trainer should be able to manage alone but if it is much bigger than 20 × 20 m (66 × 66 ft), he or she will require an assistant. When the horse first comes in, it should be encouraged to have a bit of fun and look around but obviously not allowed to roll as it has a saddle on! It will take a few minutes to settle down and it is fascinating to watch how different horses react when they first come out of the stable and are turned loose in a school.

When the initial excitement has worn off and the horse has settled down, it is then called and given a pat and a titbit. The side-reins are then attached and the session starts in earnest. Using the same vocal commands as if the horse was on the lunge, the trainer begins to work the horse forward. Because there is no contact with the horse, it is now 'body language' that has to be used to control it. By positioning yourself on either side of the centre line, one side or other of the school will become more attractive to the horse by offering a wider 'escape route'. In the early stages, this will help to keep the horse on the desired rein without a change of direction. In the later stages it will become possible to change the rein by word of command and movement across the centre line to change the 'escape route'. In the early stages the movement can be as much as a couple of metres to either side of the centre line but, eventually, the trainer will do little more than make one small step to either side of the centre line in order to produce the desired result. At no stage does loose-schooling become a matter of chasing the horse round an enclosed space with the aid of a long

A horse working loose in an indoor school.

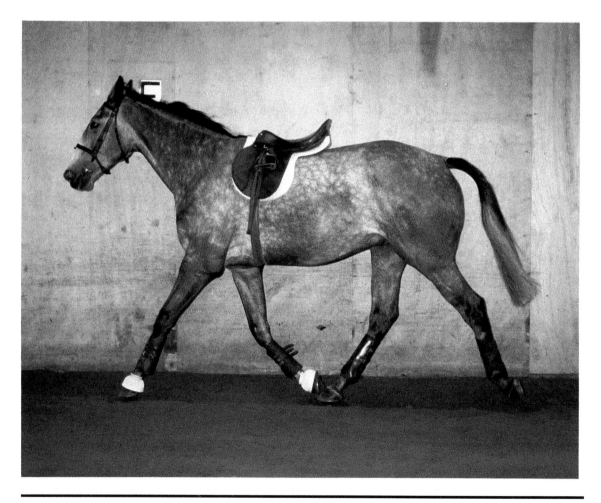

whip. This is not loose-schooling, it is mere bullying and frightening of the horse. Properly executed, loose-schooling by a quiet and sympathetic trainer is most rewarding. Chasing the horse will always be detrimental to training.

I like to introduce canter while the horse is loose as it will normally offer it without being asked. Horses usually show a preference for working alongside a wall, so the horse should stay well out on a large circle. This will make it easier for it to keep its balance on circles and corners. This type of training forms a close bond between pupil and trainer through the horse wishing to come to the trainer without being forced and being rewarded for doing so.

These sessions should not exceed 20 minutes. At the end of a session, all the equipment can be removed and the horse allowed to have a roll and cool off and relax before returning to its stable. In many show-jumping yards the young horses are introduced to poles on the ground and other small obstacles during these loose-schooling periods. More information about suitable obstacles is given in Chapter 9.

Horses have wonderful memories and one example that illustrates this concerns a horse that had been loose-schooled as a youngster by Mr Tilke, former proprietor and founder of the Windmill Hill Riding Academy in Stratford-on-Avon where I trained as a BHSAI (British Horse Society Assistant Instructor). He was to give a demonstration of loose-schooling for the local Riding Club one evening and had asked the owner of one particular horse if he could use it. He had not seen it for over a year and, prior to the demonstration, had not visited it where it was stabled overnight. His first encounter with his former equine pupil took place in the arena in front of the audience. The horse knew him immediately, whinnied loudly and rushed over to him. The horse proceeded to do everything that was required of him and then left, continuing to whinny all the way up the drive! It just goes to prove what a tremendous bond of friendship can be formed through the mutual respect established from the basis of correct training. This demonstration was most impressive and influenced many of the audience to take up loose-schooling as part of their own breaking process.

## THE FIRST FEW WEEKS AFTER BREAKING

Lungeing of the horse before any ridden schooling off the lunge should continue for the first few weeks. This is done only for about five minutes on each rein to get the horse warmed up and to make sure its muscles are relaxed before having to carry the weight of the rider.

During these first few weeks, it is advisable to have an older horse to follow so that the aids do not have to be given too strongly. Trot should always be done rising, with the rider leaning forward so that he or she is sitting as lightly as possible. The hands should be low and on each side of the neck, giving a sympathetic feeling to the horse. If the horse becomes tense or anxious the rider must take hold of the neck strap, sit up and tighten the knees. The automatic reaction is to pull on the reins but this will only cause the horse to panic, increase speed and possibly buck. It is very detrimental for the education of a young horse if the rider gets bucked off as this does actually frighten the horse if not the rider as well! If it does happen, the horse *must* be remounted immediately as if it discovers that by removing this unpleasant weight from its back it gets to stop work, it will soon decide that this is a good idea. This is why only a secure, experienced person should ride young horses, especially in the beginning.

When the young horse is first ridden off the lunge it may be wise to have someone standing nearby.

At first, just aim to sit lightly and confidently on the horse. Follow a more experienced horse and start introducing the aids at the same time as using the voice. Use the same vocal commands that were used on the lunge but do not talk continuously. By following the older horse, you are using the natural herd instinct of the young horse. Once the horse understands what the aids mean, it will have to learn to go on its own.

The immature young horse should not be subjected to strong back aids from the rider, which should only be applied in later stages of training. The object of strong back aids is to bring the hindquarters down and the hind legs under the horse to improve its balance and lighten its forehand. If these aids are applied too early in its training, far from encouraging the horse to round its back and engage its hindquarters, the opposite reaction will be a more likely result. The immature horse will hollow its back and trail its hindquarters more excessively, will not engage its hocks and quarters in downward transitions and its weight will be transferred on to its forelegs. In most cases, strong back aids should not be applied until at least a year after breaking. The more massive the framework of the horse and the more muscular its development is, as in European warmblood horses, the earlier the acceptance of strong back aids can be expected. The more lightly framed English Thoroughbred or three-quarter-bred horse will require a longer period of time to mature to the point where strong back aids can be applied.

During the latter stages of its work with a companion, the young pupil should be encouraged to take the lead position and precede the companion. It can then progress to the stage where it will turn off the track and start to work on its own, although with the companion still in the arena. This allows an easy transition to working entirely on its own without the presence of a companion. This is also an early lesson in accustoming the horse to leave its companions when its rider requires it to do so.

## MOUNTING

Although the rider will need to be given a leg up while still leaning over the horse and when they first ride it, mounting properly must also be taught during the early stages of training.

Ask an assistant to hold the horse's head and the offside stirrup iron and then place a mounting box alongside the horse. This box will probably have been used earlier when the horse was getting accustomed to being patted and touched all over. The nearside stirrup iron must then be turned so that the rider's toe will be nowhere near the girth. Keeping the toe well down, the rider will step up and lightly lower themselves down into the saddle. It is vital

that the rider's toe does not touch the horse as this could cause an explosion at that point and make the horse difficult to mount throughout its life. The saddle must not be pulled or dragged down at one side as this will not only worry the horse, but will damage the saddle and probably the horse's back as well. The rider must constantly remember the necessity to make all movements controlled and the transference of weight as light as possible. Dragging on the saddle when stepping up and slumping into the sitting position must be avoided at all costs.

Always mount from some kind of mounting block at this stage of training. After the first few times, the assistant can stand a little way off. Eventually, with a long stirrup leather and an assistant holding the other stirrup, you can mount from the ground but this should not be done too often as it puts a strain on the young horse's back.

Always be very careful when mounting.

## PROBLEMS

Obviously, problems can occur during the early stages of breaking, especially with nervous, highly strung horses or ones that have been mishandled. The worst horses are those that an inexperienced person has started breaking and then stopped because they have come up against a problem which they have been unable to solve. One problem that the modern world has inflicted upon us is lack of time. These days, everything can be produced and despatched in a quarter of the time that it used to take — except horses. Some owners want the job completed as soon as possible, so you must explain before you start that the 'riding away' stage can take anything from a week to six weeks or even longer. If you are a professional trainer, it is probably best to suggest six weeks as being the necessary time. Should the horse prove to be a quick and easy learner and the job is completed in less time, you will be heralded as a genius. If the horse is a slow or obstinate animal and your one week becomes six weeks, however good a job you do you will be dubbed either a failure or somebody who is spinning out the job to earn extra income.

### Nervous Horses

Most of these horses are usually nervous due to lack of handling before they are sent for breaking. It will require time and patience to gain their confidence. Put them in a stable near other horses, preferably in a busy part of the yard. Each time anyone passes the stable, they should make an effort to speak kindly to the horse and, if possible, try to touch and handle it.

Some horses, which have led a very sheltered life and have only been handled by one person, can be very frightened and apprehensive of strangers. We had one that we had to corner in the stable, using a show-jump pole, in order to catch it! Its owner had assured us that it was quiet and well handled but it had never left home. We kept a headcollar on it all the time so that we could catch it without frightening it further. Another one had never had a half stable door and was very worried about being able to see out. He never really recovered from this and even as a mature competition horse he never looked out over his door. Both of these horses were given time before anything more than leading about in hand and handling them all over was done. They always remained sharp in their reactions but, then, this is what makes a good competition horse. The moral of these stories is take what you are told with a pinch of salt and come to your own conclusions.

A nervous horse should be lunged with stirrup leathers, tied-up lunge reins, etc. dangling from the saddle. This will get it used to things moving and banging before the rider to tries to mount.

## A Headshy Horse

Some horses are nervous around their heads, especially their ears. In this case, it may be necessary to use a bridle that has a buckle in the headpiece so that it can be done up without sliding it over the ears. Again, this problem can arise due to lack of handling or unsympathetic handling and it will best be rectified by regular fondling.

Two-year-old colts can be very naughty about biting and may box with their front legs. If they are controlled by being smacked around the head, they soon become headshy. Unfortunately, this often happens in Thoroughbred studs where potential racehorses are left entire in case they become stars in their racing careers and can then be retired to stud.

## Mounting

This is the most likely time for problems to occur. I had one client who sent me horses on a regular basis, having been 'broken but just needed to be backed'. Some horses are just nervous about having someone higher than themselves. In this case, spend a lot of time standing on something and being taller than the horse. Sacks of straw can be hung from the rafters in the stable so that the horse becomes used to pushing between things that are above it. In the old days, a contraption called a dumb jockey was used. This comprised a wooden cross, with sacks of straw tied to it to make a body and arms, which was tied to the saddle. The legs were onion sacks filled with sand, which dangled down on each side. Another onion bag filled with sand was tied over the saddle to increase the weight. It was vital that this contraption was tied securely to the saddle and could not be removed by bucking. If you have a horse that does not like someone above it, something like this could be tried. The horse can then buck, rear or whatever it likes without dislodging its 'rider'. It will soon realize that there is nothing to be alarmed about and will, in time, accept a real rider rather than a dummy one.

A horse that has learnt to buck an unwanted weight off its back is also a problem. The Indian method (described on p.7) of taking it into deep water is quite effective. One of Great Britain's better known three day event horses had to be mounted in this way, having injured several riders by depositing them unceremoniously on the ground!

If the horse becomes nervous at any time during mounting, it must be taken back to a stage where it is happy and confident. When training has been completed in a methodical manner this should be straightforward. Progress in all aspects of training must be made at a speed suitable to the temperament and ability of the horse to avoid unnecessary confrontations.

## Dismounting

Some horses become frightened by someone dismounting. This can be because they have been touched by the rider's right leg as they lifted it over the quarters, if there has been a sudden movement of the rider's body or if the horse has moved and the rider falls, rather than jumps, off. It is a very awkward problem as the horse then begins to jump sideways as you are going to dismount. The way around this is to ask an assistant to hold the horse's head in a corner with its body along a wall. It cannot then jump forwards or sideways and the rider can dismount in the orthodox manner. The lesson of dismounting must be repeated several times.

# BASIC TRAINING

It is obviously the aim of every trainer to produce a horse that is completely obedient to the aids. In order to achieve this, the first requirement is a horse that is well balanced, supple and has a responsive mouth.

Education has already started on the lunge. Whatever role the horse or pony is to have in later life, an obedient horse will increase the pleasure and success to be gained from riding it. Obedience comes when there is total trust and respect on both sides. As with any animal, mutual harmony between horse and rider cannot be achieved by bullying or aggression but only through patient, yet firm, handling.

Horses, like children, must have some discipline but must not be ruled with a rod of iron so that it produces rebellion or a complete obliteration of spirit. On the other hand, they must not be spoilt as this produces a thoroughly obnoxious and, in most cases, useless and dangerous animal. As with children, the difficult part is to strike a happy medium.

The basic training will be the same in the early stages no matter what activity is the final objective of the trainer. Not many years ago, this was not true of the racing world, which tended to adopt a rough, ready and quick system when backing and introducing the horse to its work. There were many casualties among the pupils, who suffered from strained tendons and joints and badly affected temperaments. There were also quite a few casualties among the unfortunates who had been legged up on to their backs.

One of the pioneers in the introduction of proper schooling and training of young horses in racing stables was Robert Hall of dressage fame. With the co-operation of a racehorse trainer, he demonstrated that basic dressage training was beneficial, both

A Thoroughbred horse's passport, showing its date of birth and parentage.

**THE STUD BOOK AUTHORITY OF GREAT BRITAIN & IRELAND**

**WEATHERBYS, SANDERS ROAD, WELLINGBOROUGH,**

**NORTHANTS, NN8 4BX.**

Document of description of the identification of produce, race-horses, brood mares and stallions.

(Livret signalétique pour l'identification des produits des chevaux de course, des mères et des pères.)

Issued on behalf of the Turf Authorities and the Stud Book Authority. (Etabli au nom des Autorités Hippiques et au nom de L'autorité de Stud Book)

| PASSPORT No. (No. de PASSEPORT) | 832734 | AUTHORISED STAMP | JE |
|---|---|---|---|
| NAME (NOM) | INT' SIN BIN | | |
| YEAR OF FOALING (Anneé de Naissance) | 1979 | | |
| COUNTRY OF BIRTH (PAYS DE NAISSANCE) | IRELAND | | |
| STUD BOOK REF. (Reference Au Stud Book) | VOL 39 G.S.B. | | |
| COLOUR (ROBE) | BAY | | |
| SEX (SEXE) | GELDING | | |
| SIRE (PERE) | PAUPER | | |
| DAM (MERE) | KILVELLANE CHERRY | | |
| G SIRE (G PERE) | RAISE YOU TEN | | |

from a performance point of view and for avoidance of future veterinary problems. Over the years more and more racing establishments have adopted proper basic training and paid more attention to the physical development of their young charges. Sadly, though, this is not yet true of all trainers.

After the basic schooling has been completed, it will be time to decide where the pupil's talent, and therefore its best chance of success, lies. To be successful, the horse or pony will need to follow a course of training that it finds relatively easy. In Germany there is a highly specialized breeding programme, which means that a horse is bred from particular parents so that it has the required genes to do a specific job. Of course, there is always the occasional one that is bred for dressage but, instead, shows a talent for jumping or vice versa – they are the exception that proves the rule! In Britain breeders are becoming more aware of the desirability of specialized breeding as the demands of competition rise, but we still have a long way to go. The Worshipful Company of Saddlers and the British Horse Foundation have recently combined forces to produce a computerized database for the national registration of horses and ponies. This will make it possible to link breeding stock with performance results and will take much of the mystery out of breeding and buying, thus bringing Britain into line with other European countries. Even so, there are many excellent eventers, show jumpers and dressage horses who come from impeccable Thoroughbred family trees but are too slow to race. There is a very true saying: 'Fools breed horses for wise men to buy!'

Schooling the horse needs to be divided into separate stages, the final goal being an all-round athlete. There is no specific rule as to how long these stages will take to complete and the next step should only be taken when the previous goal has been achieved. There will be no *exact* moment when it is correct to proceed and the progression should always be gradual. There are no short cuts as these will only reveal themselves later in training.

## COMMUNICATION

Communication between the horse and rider is achieved by the use of the aids which are the signals or language by which the rider conveys their wishes to the horse, who has been taught to understand and obey them. The aids are split into two groups:

* natural aids;
* artificial aids.

The natural aids are the rider's legs, hands, voice and body weight transferred through the seat. This latter aid must be light and sympathetic when applied to the immature horse. The artificial aids are sticks, spurs and martingales. As previously mentioned, a dressage or schooling whip may be used with a young horse but none of the other artificial aids should be necessary. Response to the aids will start in the stable when the horse is nudged with the fingers at the same time as being told 'Over!' by the voice. These lessons continue as the horse is lunged, when it is controlled by the voice, backed up by the correct use of the lunge whip. This part of the training is very important as it will develop the horse's awareness to 'touch', at first accompanied by the voice and later without it.

When the young horse is first ridden, it will not respond to the leg aids. To introduce it to this new signal, you must nudge with your legs at the same time as using your voice. Always carry a schooling whip so that, if the aid is ignored, a flick from the end of the whip, just behind your leg, will reinforce the command. When the horse does respond, pat it and praise it verbally. Gradually, as the horse begins to understand these signals, the use of the voice can be stopped.

## TRAINING

The young horse should not be ridden for too long at any one time. Its education on the lunge should continue and it can then be ridden at the end of the session before it tires. If it is asked for more than it is physically able to do or ridden when its muscles are tired, it will stiffen up and resist. At the beginning, it is educational for the horse to be mounted and dismounted and asked to stand still with and without a helper. Lungeing, loose-schooling and being led near farm machinery or farm animals are all educational. The young horse has to be introduced to life in the outside world.

## SCHOOLING

Schooling must not only be thought of as periods of correction. Instead, it comprises periods of learning and achievement, especially in the case of the young horse.

Each session should last for about 15 minutes or so for the first week, increasing to 30 minutes as the horse becomes stronger. These sessions should only include walk and rising trot. Once the young horse has begun to understand the aids, riding it with other horses, so that it is sometimes following another horse, sometimes leading and constantly having to circle away, is very beneficial.

A word of warning should be given here. If the pupil is always accompanied by the same equine companion, a relationship can be built up between the two that will be hard to overcome later. The result can often be seen in horses from small yards, when the removal of one horse, perhaps to jump its round in a competition, causes its companion to call or even to try to demolish its trailer or box. Not only can this lead to damage to both horse and equipment, it will also distract the ridden horse, causing loss of concentration and even nappiness. It is therefore of benefit to work both the trained and the half-trained horse separately on occasions.

The voice becomes used less as the horse improves. During this stage the horse is asked to perform large circles of not less than 20 m (66 ft) in diameter and progressive transitions, both upward and downward, from halt to trot. The aim is to have the horse carrying the rider happily in walk and trot.

## TURNING THE THREE-YEAR-OLD AWAY

Choosing the time to turn the young horse out after its initial backing will depend largely on the maturity of the youngster. Having always had more to do with Thoroughbred or Thoroughbred-cross horses, I prefer to bring them to the stage where they are reasonably responsive and then turn them away so that they can have six weeks or so in the field before the weather breaks for winter. During this time they are out all the time, weather permitting, are fed all the hay they will eat and are given two feeds of yearling cubes each day. The important thing is that their education must be progressing well before they are turned away. They will then think about what they have been doing while they are resting and come in again bigger, stronger and going even better. If they have had a problem before going out, they will come in bigger, stronger and with a more established problem!

Field management while youngsters are out should follow all the rules of good, safe fencing, some form of shelter and a fresh supply of water. Grass should have been properly looked after and regular checks made for poisonous plants. Remember that young animals can only fully develop physically when they are kept warm and safe and fed well. If these young horses have their rest during the autumn, it will be beneficial in several ways:

- they are not left to run wild for too long and therefore will not need rebreaking when they come back into work;
- they can work through the winter and be introduced to all sorts of new experiences while being kept warm and well fed;
- they will be ready for another break in the spring, as four-year-olds, when the grass is coming through.

If it is decided to go on further with the training while the weather is still good and to turn the young horse away through the winter, it must be well fed throughout and brought into either a stable or a yard at night.

## BASIC TRAINING OF THE FOUR-YEAR-OLD

The aims of the basic training are to maintain calmness, encourage free forward movement, establish rhythm and have the horse completely straight throughout.

Calmness is usually easier to obtain from the younger horse, once it has accepted the saddle, than from the older horse, who can easily become excited and tense. Once a young horse has had its mind stimulated by outside activities, such as going to a show, it may be different! It is important for the horse to remain calm because then its muscles are relaxed and its natural paces and way of going can be developed.

Each schooling session must begin with a warming-up or loosening phase. It is unnatural for the horse to stand in a stable for long periods and the muscles will become stiff. If the young horse is lunged for 10 to 15 minutes before the rider mounts, this should be sufficient to relax it.

The first five minutes of lungeing should be carried out without having the side-reins attached so that the horse can stretch downwards and forwards. If the rider mounts the horse immediately, it is important to get the horse working forward, long and low, so that its back is loose. It is important that it is not allowed to take its balance from the rider's hand and stop working from behind. If the horse is allowed to stay in this long, low outline, on its forehand and with no impulsion from behind, it will lose all the natural sparkle from its paces. To avoid this result, the rider must employ hand and leg, correctly balancing the one with the other. Equally, the horse must be schooled to accept this way of going.

## CONTACT

To understand the term 'riding on a contact', it may be helpful to draw an anology with the use of a garden hose. If a gardener wishes to water a lawn, he or she will first turn on the tap and the water then flows out of the end of the hose, narrowly missing their boots.

In the absence of a nozzle, the gardener partially blocks the end of the hose with a thumb and the water immediately forms a jet which greatly increases the range. If, however, they put their thumb too firmly over the end of the hose, the water squirts in all directions except the desired one or the pipe bursts or becomes detached from the tap.

So it is when riding a horse on a contact. 'The tap' is turned on by the application of the leg aids. If there is no contact, the horse's weight goes on to its forehand, the energy is lost and, in some cases, even forward movement may be lost. Too much restriction from the hand may give rise to disobedience or rebellion but, in either case, will stop forward movement. A correct degree of contact, which allows as well as restricts, will produce a light and energetic pace.

## THE GAITS

The horse has four gaits although there are variations within each one.

### Walk

Walk is a gait in four-time, which means that the horse puts each foot on the ground individually. The sequence of footfalls is:

1  left (near) hind;
2  left (near) front;
3  right (off) hind;
4  right (off) front.

The steps must be even and regular with a distinct marching beat. The walk is the most delicate of all the gaits and is easily spoiled by bad riding, that is, by stiffness and/or restriction from the rider's hands, being forced into a 'collected outline' or unsteady hand aids. Once the walk steps have been destroyed, it is virtually impossible to put things right. The walk has four categories:

- free;
- medium;
- collected;
- extended.

Young horses enjoying a break in the field after their initial training.

The sequence of footfalls.

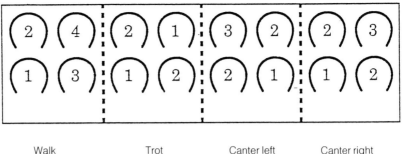

Walk          Trot          Canter left     Canter right

*Free Walk*

This is used during the first stages of a warm-up period, especially in an enclosed training area, such as an indoor school or a small, well-fenced paddock. It allows the horse the freedom to stretch and lower its head and neck and encourages suppleness in the muscles after a time of inactivity in the stable. The other important use of the free walk is as a reward after energetic exercise, such as a dressage test or a steeplechase course.

The free walk allows the horse to stretch and lower its neck because a long rein is allowed by the rider. Free walk can be performed with either a long rein or a loose rein. The difference between the two is that on a long rein the rider maintains a light contact with the horse's mouth but does not seek to influence the position of head or neck. A long rein is usually best used in warm-up periods. A loose rein involves no rider contact and is, as its name implies, a slack rein, allowing complete freedom to the horse apart from an occasional touch for steering. This rein is best used as a reward for the physically tired horse.

During training and exercise sessions, riding on a loose rein and riding on a contact should both be practised and any tendency of the horse to anticipate trot, because of the resumption of a contact, must be corrected otherwise that most annoying of habits, jogging, will result whenever the rider alters their hand position.

*Medium Walk*

This is the pace normally used for working the horse. The steps must be positive and regular, covering the ground well, energetic and rhythmical. The horse is ridden on a contact that must be allowing and sympathetic. Above all, it must not be restrictive. If lungeing has been properly carried out with correctly adjusted side-reins, the horse will already have begun to acquire the first stages of an 'outline'. It should be the aim of the trainer to reproduce this way of going in the transition to manual rein control and, in due course, to improve upon it.

*Collected Walk*

This is an Advanced movement. The whole outline of the horse is shortened and the weight is taken right back on to the hocks so that the forehand rises at the withers, with the head and poll arched. The steps remain full of impulsion but the hind legs step right under the horse into the print of the forefoot or just in front of it.

Collection must be achieved through the creation of the energy in the horse's hindquarters being contained by the rider's hand, *not* by the rider's hand pulling the forehand backwards.

*Extended Walk*

The horse is allowed to make a longer outline so that it may take as long a step as possible. In allowing the horse to lengthen its head and neck, the contact on the mouth must still be maintained. The steps must lengthen, not quicken, in the attempt to achieve extension. It must be remembered that, except in extreme circumstances of self-preservation, the horse cannot extend its toe in front of an imaginary vertical line drawn through its nose to the ground. Thus the importance of allowing the lengthening of head and neck becomes obvious.

## Trot

Trot is a two-time gait, which means that the horse uses its legs in diagonal pairs. There are two steps to a stride. The sequence is:

1   left (near) fore and right (off) hind together;
2   right (off) fore and left (near) hind together.

There is a brief moment of suspension between each step, during which there are no feet on the ground. It is from this two-time gait that rising trot comes. The rider will rise when one pair of legs is on the ground and sit in the saddle when the other pair comes to the ground. Sitting trot must only be executed by riders who are supple enough to absorb the movement of the trot and on horses that are strong enough to carry the rider's weight. The trot also has variations of the basic pace:

- working;
- medium;
- collected;
- extended.

*Working Trot*

This is what the name suggests and is the trot used for most of the young horse's training. The steps should be longer than those of collected trot and the horse must be going freely forward, maintaining balance and rhythm.

### Medium Trot

This is halfway between working and extended trot. The impulsion is increased but the round outline is maintained. The nose is allowed a little in front of the vertical to allow the steps to lengthen.

### Collected Trot

The hind legs are well engaged, lightening and raising the forehand, as in the walk. The back must remain loose and supple and the horse must remain relaxed in the contact. Any restriction or anxiety will spoil the movement and the horse will not give the impression of being light and freely mobile.

### Extended Trot

This is just an extension of medium trot. It is the trot with the longest stride and the greatest amount of impulsion.

## Canter

This is a three-time gait. The sequence of the canter for left canter is:

1  right (off) hind;
2  left (near) hind and right (off) fore *together*;
3  left (near) fore.

There is a moment of suspension at the end of each sequence, when all four feet are off the ground.

The canter has similar variations of pace to the trot:

- working;
- medium;
- collected;
- extended.

The definitions are also similar. Collected canter has shorter steps but greater impulsion than working canter, and is only used by more advanced horses. Working canter is the pace used for 'working'. Medium canter has stronger, bolder steps with more impulsion but the outline of the horse remains the same. Extended canter is a stage further, where the steps are at their maximum length, with maximum impulsion, while still maintaining rhythm, balance and outline.

## Gallop

This is a four-time gait. The sequence of the gallop is:

1  right (off) hind;
2  left (near) hind;
3  right (off) fore;
4  left (near) fore.

There is also a period of suspension at the end of each sequence.

## FREE-FORWARD MOVEMENT

Once the horse is being ridden away from the security of the lunge, it must be ridden positively foward. The horse is a herd animal and it is totally unnatural for it to work away from friends or home. It must be reassured and encouraged to go where it is told so that it develops trust and confidence in its rider. If the horse misunderstands the rider's wishes and needs correction, this must be applied sympathetically but also firmly. Too harsh a correction or too lenient a reaction on the part of the rider may lead to serious problems in later stages of training. It is vital that the horse and rider 'think' forwards and that the horse will respond 'forwards' to the leg aid. It must be remembered that horses, just like humans, have to learn what is meant by certain signals. For any upward transition or forward aid, the rider's leg should operate on the girth. This is because a nerve called the intercostal nerve is nearest to the surface of the skin in this area. The horse is more sensitive here because touching this nerve has a rounding effect on the lumbar muscles in its back. The rider's hand must allow the horse to move forward and not restrict it in any way. Obviously, of course, if the horse rushes forward, a correction has to be made but there must be no snatching on the rein by the rider as then the horse will be confused because it went forward as asked and then was stopped, so what was the rider actually wanting? The correction should be as gentle as possible while still achieving obedience.

The downward transition is made with a different leg aid in conjunction with a 'tweak' on the outside rein. In this case, the leg is used as a 'holding' leg so that the horse's hocks stay underneath it and it can 'sit' on them and retain its balance. The rider's leg aids must be quite distinguishable so that the horse understands that an urgent, nudging aid means 'go on', while a holding leg means 'steady' and 'slow down'.

The very green, young horse will have no idea what is expected of it. The same vocal aids used when it was on the lunge should now be employed in conjunction with the use of the leg. It is also helpful to have someone with a lunge whip standing in the middle of the schooling area. The horse will soon begin to associate the voice with the leg aids. Like children, young horses absorb knowledge like a sponge but this also means that they learn everything – right or wrong. Obviously, the wrong ideas must be avoided as much as possible. The rider must try to 'think like the horse', anticipate how it will react in a certain circumstance and prevent an undesirable response rather than having to correct a wrong action.

The horse must be encouraged to go forward from the rider's leg aids.

Once the young horse is going forward in the school and is sufficiently responsive to the basic aids, it can be taken out for rides in the company of another, sensible horse. This will give the youngster more of an interest in what is going on and the other horse will give it the support and courage to go foward. This habit of forward going and forward thinking must be established before any serious demands are made, going in a rounded shape.

## RHYTHM

Out in the field a young horse has a certain amount of natural balance but when the weight of a rider is put on its back this is lost. Its own weight then falls forward and puts an extra strain on the forelegs. It is therefore the duty of the rider to get the horse working comfortably within its own balance so that a regular rhythm can be established. Obviously, a load that is distributed evenly will be easier to carry than one that is not, so it is imperative that the horse learns to take its weight equally on all four legs.

Rhythm is usually first established in trot as this is the easiest gait in which to establish a definite beat as it is in two-time. All the horse has to do is swing along from one diagonal to the other. It is vital at this stage that the rider frequently changes the diagonal that they ride on so that the muscles in the horse's back develop equally. We all have a favourite diagonal on which to rise and a concentrated effort must be made to change so that the horse does not become stiff and one-sided. It is easier to ride the horse forward in rising trot so that the 'forward attitude' is maintained.

Riding to music will help the horse and rider to find a rhythm and keep it. Music also helps to induce relaxation and brings a regular tempo to the work. Some years ago we had a young Thoroughbred horse that would shuffle along until he could catch the rhythm of the music and then he would be away – transformed from an unlevel cripple into a beautiful and graceful mover. It is enjoyable for both parties and adds a little gaiety to the repetitive work required at the beginning of any young horse's training.

Working the horse long and low will encourage its back to swing and become soft and supple but it must not be allowed to 'collapse' on to its forehand. It will take many months to strengthen the hindquarters and make them strong enough to carry the weight back. Obviously, smaller, shorter-coupled horses take less time to become better balanced than longer, gangly ones.

The canter is normally the next pace to improve. As the work in trot becomes more rhythmical and balanced, the canter rhythm will automatically get better. Walk is the most difficult gait and is usually the last to develop. In the beginning stages of the walk, the horse should be ridden on a long rein so that the steps are not spoiled. Much of this work can be done out on a hack so that the walk will develop naturally.

## SIMPLE EXERCISES

Schooling in a manège at this stage will involve the riding of large circles, changes of rein and transitions. The circles will ensure that the inside hind leg has to step underneath the horse. These circles must not be less than 20 m (66 ft) in diameter as circles that are too small will cause strain, loss of balance and stiffness. This may even lead to a lifetime inability to circle correctly. The rider must use the inside leg on the girth to maintain the foward movement while pushing the horse out on the circle. The outside leg will be drawn slightly behind the girth to control the hindquarters and therefore encourage the horse to bend.

At this point the term 'bend' must be properly understood. The horse has a backbone which, while it is able to round or hollow on a vertical plane, has little or no ability to bend laterally. What we refer to as 'bending' is, in fact, an optical illusion. The horse *is* able to make a slight contraction between the ribs to the inside of a circle and a corresponding extension of the rubs on the outside of the circle. In addition, if the rider's inside leg is being applied correctly, the horse's inside hind leg will be brought further under the horse and the shoulder will move slightly back. Combined with a slight lateral curve of head and neck, the illusion of bend is thus created. Using the inside leg on the girth activates the

*Left* 20-m (22-yd) circle.

*Centre* Showing a correct bend to the right while on a circle to the right.

*Right* Serpentine.

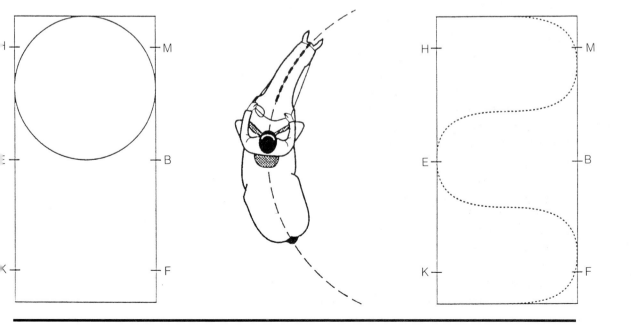

intercostal nerve which can also spark off a spontaneous signal to the muscles under the lumbar vertebrae so that they stretch and arch above the spine at the same time as the inside hind leg is carried underneath the body.

Using their inside leg in this manner, in conjunction with a steady rein contact on the outside rein, the rider will encourage the horse to obtain a good balance. Any restriction on the inside rein will cramp the muscles on the inside and prevent the inside hind leg from coming through. This feeling has been aptly described as like riding down a tunnel. If the reins are attached to the tunnel walls and the inside rein is pulled, it will close the tunnel!

Transitions and changes of rein will help to accustom the horse to altering its balance in order to carry itself and its rider. The rider must be very careful to sit in a secure position over the horse's centre of gravity in order to help the horse obtain its objective. The naturally well balanced horse will find these exercises much easier than a less talented horse.

When the horse is young and unbalanced, it is vital that only an experienced rider is employed. The rider must be capable of offering balance and stability to a young horse that lacks these qualities. A less-experienced rider could well add to the horse's problems if balance and the continuity of aids are not maintained. The rider's demands must be tempered by an understanding of the pupil's current ability, both physical and mental. A demand that is made too harshly or is too advanced for the pupil's stage of training, can lead to rebellion. It is also important that the rider's seat remains light, to allow the horse's back to round. As soon as the young horse shows signs of being tired, the training session must stop. The wise trainer will anticipate the horse's tiredness and will finish the session at the first opportunity of ending on a good note. Through lack of anticipation, the foolish trainer will carry on until the horse is obviously too tired to produce the desired result and the lesson may end at a point where uncorrected disobedience has occurred. Training sessions should always end on a successful note.

To establish rhythm, the rider must be able to ride with a good contact on the rein so that the forward movement is contained and cadence and rhythm are developed in the paces of the horse.

## STRAIGHTNESS

The horse must always be straight, whether it is travelling in a straight line, through a corner or round a circle. This may sound contradictory. Here, 'straightness' means that the hind legs must follow in the tracks of the forelegs. For this to happen on a bend, the inside hind leg must take a shorter, higher stride than the outside

The horse's work must be varied and should include going out for hacks in the countryside.

hind leg and therefore bend the hock more. If this does not happen, the horse will trail its hocks and lose impulsion or swing its hindquarters out – either action will result in a loss of rhythm.

It is extremely difficult for the young horse to go in a straight line as horses are naturally crooked: usually they are bent slightly to the left and there are two schools of thought on the reason for this:

- Museler suggests that the unborn foal is usually curled to the left in the mare's womb before it is born;
- all handling of the young horse is done from the left-hand side.

The aim throughout training must be to make the horse supple to both sides and evenly responsive. It will be impossible for it to remain in balance and rhythm unless it can push equally with each hind leg. It will learn to do this on circles, when each hind leg takes its turn being on the inside and being the weight-bearing leg.

At this stage the rider must be very aware of where their weight is placed. Because the horse's inside hind leg is its weight-carrying leg, the rider's weight must be positioned over this leg.

At this stage the schooling sessions should continue using circles, shallow loops with and without circles, serpentines and transitions to supple the horse and to help to teach straightness. All schooling sessions must be enjoyable for both horse and rider and not become boring as this will induce dullness. The lessons must be made as interesting and as varied as the weather and facilities allow. If an indoor school is used often, work must also be done in an outdoor arena or a field. The horse must pursue all aspects of training by going for hacks, doing polework, jumping and going across country. Only when it has mastered the rules of basic training will it be able to specialize in the particular field for which it shows an aptitude.

Throughout the simple exercises mentioned above, the horse must be worked with sufficient energy to bring the hocks underneath the body. As the training progresses, they will have to come further and further under the body for the horse to be able to execute the more advanced exercises. Smaller circles will demand increasing flexibility of the inside hind leg. Continuous changes of direction, as in serpentines or shallow loops, make the horse change the weight-bearing leg quickly as well as changing the bend, thus suppling the horse.

## TURN ON THE FOREHAND

Turn on the forehand is a training exercise that is used to introduce both horse and rider to lateral work. In this movement the horse is asked to move its hindquarters around the front legs, which remain marking time on the spot. The inside hind leg

A turn on the forehand showing how the horse's inside hind leg crosses in front of the outside hind leg.

crosses in front of the outside hind leg, making an arc around the forehand while maintaining the rhythm of the walk. The turn is named after the slight bend that is asked for at the horse's poll, i.e. a left turn is when the horse is looking slightly to the left and moving away from the rider's left leg.

The aids for left turn on the forehand are: the rider's left leg used in a nudging manner, asking for, rather than demanding, a movement away from the leg. A strong and abrupt aid may cause the horse to move forward, which is contrary to the concept of the movement. A soft, pushing aid will encourage the horse to yield to the pressure and give way without any sudden movement. The horse's hindquarters could be said to be 'stroked' into lateral movement. The rider's right leg is used to regulate the speed of the turn and also helps to stop the exercise when it is completed. This leg plays its part in keeping the horse up into the bridle and is also held in readiness to prevent any backward movement of the horse. The inside rein indicates the direction of the bend, while the outside rein controls the amount of bend and the outside shoulder. Both legs help to maintain the impulsion and to prevent the horse from stepping backwards, while both reins have a restraining influence and prevent the horse from moving forwards.

Before attempting the movement, a suitable place must be selected. If it is to be performed in an arena, the horse must be brought in away from the wall so that enough room is left for the head and neck. The horse's quarters must always move towards the inside of the arena so that the horse is *never* encouraged to swing its hindquarters out.

Apart from teaching the horse to move away from the rider's leg, this is an invaluable exercise in the education of the rider. It teaches him or her to use their leg in a different manner from the 'nudge, nudge, get up and go' aid which is all that has been necessary up to this stage. Before any lateral, or sideways, work can be attempted, the 'pushing over' leg aid must be mastered. Co-ordination of the aids and a 'feel' for the horse's rhythm are also lessons that can be learnt from this exercise.

The horse must stay in a rounded outline and take big steps, one at a time. Each step must be taken deliberately after a single push from the rider's inside leg. The horse must never run away in tiny sidesteps at a rate of knots, as this defeats the object of the exercise. Every step should be the result of an applied leg aid, not a rush sideways away from continuous pressure. It must never be forgotten that the horse must *always* think and go forward even though the direction of the movement is sideways.

Turn on the forehand is a movement that is easily taught to both horse and rider. As a result, riders tend to overuse it as it is 'ego boosting' to show off to friends and relatives one's ability to turn the horse's hindquarters on a whim. Unfortunately, constant repetition will lead to a tendency for the horse to put its weight forward whenever it is asked to turn and this can have dire consequences. While turn on the forehand is a useful lesson when introducing a horse to lateral movement, it must be understood that it can also have detrimental effects when teaching the horse to make correct and balanced turns. Once the horse has understood the significance of the 'pushing leg aid', turn on the forehand should no longer be practised.

Although the movement is much vaunted as a necessary part of gate opening, I have never found it in the least bit helpful – full lateral movement, yes; turn on the forehand, no. Turn on the forehand entails the front legs marking time on the spot, which precludes the possibility of a gate swinging on its hinges. Either the gate remains shut or an unrecognized 'shuffle' and a certain amount of waltzing to the side will result. This is certainly not turn on the forehand!

## ENLARGING THE CIRCLE AWAY FROM THE INSIDE LEG

Once the horse has mastered the idea of moving away from the leg rather than increasing impulsion, it can be asked to enlarge a circle. This is done simply by taking the horse on a slightly smaller circle, for example, a 15-m (50-ft) circle, and then pushing it over with the inside leg on to a 20-m (66-ft) circle without losing the aid – initiated by the leg not the hand. The aids are similar to those used on a circle, except that the rider's inside leg will push side-ways, rather than nudge for greater impulsion. The general rule is still for the horse to remain round and take big steps sideways, crossing the inside hind leg in front of the outside hind leg.

## PROBLEMS

There are times when the training may come to a dead end because the horse has misunderstood what has been asked of it and simply switches off. If this happens, find an easier exercise to regain the horse's attention and then go back again to whatever problem had occurred. It is pointless to use force if the horse does not carry out the rider's wishes because of a lack of understanding, as this will only cause tension and anxiety on the part of the pupil.

## THE SIGNIFICANCE OF SHOEING DURING EARLY TRAINING

In the early stages of training, the young horse will only need front shoes but later, as its training progresses, it will need to be shod all round. It is sensible to put lightweight, concave, iron shoes on at first so that there is less risk of the horse injuring itself or losing its action, which quite often occurs when a youngster is first shod. Subsequently, the horse will regain its balance and become accustomed to the weight on its feet and the extra height of the shoes. When we consider the difference in the stresses on our own feet when changing from bedroom slippers to outdoor shoes – a matter of a few millimetres – the addition of half a centimetre of heavy iron to one's feet must be disconcerting in the first instance.

In these initial stages of training it is extremely important that skilful shoeing is applied. Many a young horse has been ruined by an indifferent farrier at the outset of its working life. Tendons, ligaments and bones are at their most susceptible at this early stage and untold damage can result from uninformed or inept shoeing. Obviously, the young horse must have shoes on all four feet before being taken out on to the road.

## RIDING OUT

In most rural areas, and in some enlightened urban ones, it is possible to hack out with minimal use of the roads. Unfortunately, it is becoming increasingly more difficult to find such places and the necessity of going out on the highway increases. As the roads carry ever more and faster traffic, the luxury of riding out is becoming more dangerous but it does continue to be a valuable part of the young horse's education.

Working the horse sensibly in walk and trot will help to develop its muscles and make it stronger. Canter can be also included but only in suitable areas, *not* along the grass verges. Hills can be included, not only to strengthen the horse but also to make it more agile and able to look after itself.

Before venturing out, the horse must be under control in most circumstances and must fully understand the aids but you must also appreciate that certain situations may lead to fright or panic in a youngster when confronted with strange sights or sounds. The trainer must be competent and strong enough to cope with these traumas and thus prevent horse, rider or a third party from suffering harm. In the early stages, it is advisable to go out with a sensible, experienced horse that will be able to give a lead and moral support to the youngster. The young one should be ridden on the inside of the escort horse so that it is 'protected' from the traffic and has a 'buffer' if it shies at something in the hedge. The rule in Britain is to keep to the left-hand side of the road.

It must be remembered that riding out is a whole new experience for the horse. Everything will be potentially frightening – paper bags on the grass verge, people in their gardens, dogs and, of course, all forms of traffic, especially large, rattly vehicles and lorries with air brakes. It is vital that the youngster gains confidence on these rides and is not frightened by anything as horses have very good memories and it will take a long time to repair any damage that is done. Young horses also treat the large white lettering found at road junctions with suspicion. This arises from the horse's natural, inbuilt fear of snakes, so your horse may stop dead, snort and either jump very high over the offending lettering or refuse to go past it. This is when an older horse can help, by leading your youngster past such spooky things. Of course, the young horse has to go out on its own eventually but only after it has been introduced to some of the hazards that will be encountered outside.

# PROGRESSIVE FLATWORK

## THE RIDER'S POSITION

In order to improve the horse's rhythm and balance, the rider must also achieve a good balance. With a secure position that is independent of the reins, clear aids can be given and will not become confused with involuntary signals arising out of loss of rider balance or rhythm.

A position as near as possible to that of classical equitation must be achieved so that the rider can remain in balance with the horse. The position must not, however, be obtained through rigidness or force. To achieve a good position, combined with relaxation, is easier for some types of human conformation than for others. For an instructor, if a prospective pupil enters the yard walking with toes at 'ten to two', the job of getting this pupil to ride with the correct leg position is obviously going to be very much more difficult than with a pupil who walks naturally, with their toes to the front. A true horseman can always be recognized by his footprints. In the days of the Wild West, it is said that the Indians could tell whether their adversaries were infantry or cavalry by the way their footprints pointed. The infantry man had his feet splayed; the cavalry man had his toes facing straight ahead. However, the position of the feet and legs must not be forced. The rider who is told to turn their toes to the front almost invariably creates stiffness in the ankle in trying to comply. In my experience, it is better to tell the trainee to turn the heel out, rather than the toe in, as this instruction will encourage a turning of the whole leg from the hip downwards, rather than inducing stiffness in the ankle joint and, incidently, transference of the weight in the foot from the base of the big toe, where it should be, to the base of the little toe, which tends to make the leg away from the sides to the horse.

The lower leg must be wrapped around the barrel of the horse, in contact but not gripping. Of course, over fences or in times of emergency, a certain amount of grip must be applied. At no time, however, should the lower leg be allowed to grip. The grip, such as it is, is obtained by a turning inwards of the rider's knee and thigh. Should the lower leg grip the horse, not only may the emergency be exacerbated but the rider's position will be weakened by the upward nature of the calf and ankle grip, as opposed to the downward thrust caused by turning the thigh and knee.

The length of stirrup leather, and therefore the position of the rider's lower leg and thigh, will differ according to the discipline of the contest in which he or she is riding. The dressage rider has a different requirement to the show jumper, the eventer to the show jumper, the steeplechase or flat race jockey to the eventer.

The dressage rider needs a longer leg to give precise aids.

The reasons for the alteration in leg position can be explained briefly under three headings:

- balance and the importance of the rider's aids;
- matching the horse's point of balance;
- wind resistance and overcoming natural inertia.

The dressage rider requires a long leg to give precise aids and depth of seat to employ the weight and influence of the rider's back and to look elegant. He or she does not require the ability to move at speed but does need complete control over precise and complicated movements.

The show jumper needs accurate control of the horse to negotiate turns and to lengthen or shorten the pace. This necessitates a certain length of leg but speed is of paramount importance. The faster the horse goes, the more its point of balance moves forward. A shorter leg on the rider's part will enable the point of balance to be matched, therefore a compromise must be made between the requirements of control and the requirements of speed, especially in a jump-off or a competition against the clock.

The eventer has to travel at speed during the steeplechase and cross-country phases, has to be capable of matching the horse's thrust over fences and yet travel comparatively long distances over roads and tracks without the opportunity to change saddles. The various disciplines also require specialized saddlery. The show jumper will have a very different saddle to the dressage rider as their requirements are so different, while the eventer, who requires different positions according to which phase is being tackled, will require a different design of saddle again, to accommodate their differing leg position.

To specialize at anything but the lower levels, one cannot afford to economize on equipment. At the level of pure enjoyment, it is possible to have great fun with one general purpose saddle. To get to the top in whatever discipline you select, specialized saddlery must be acquired.

The steeplechase jockey requires maximum ability to match the horse's point of balance at maximum speed, both on the flat and over the sticks. However, the jockey must still be in a position to bring the horse straight into the fence and to choose the section of the fence to be tackled. This jockey therefore needs a compromise position, with far shorter leathers than a show jumper or eventer, but still maintaining an influence on the direction the horse takes.

The flat-race jockey requires only to travel at speed, maintain a left-rein or right-rein circuit, an inside or outside position, steer for the best going and to have the courage to take advantage of a gap between the leaders. He or she also needs to know something

The flat-race jockey needs a shorter length of stirrup to match the horse's point of balance at maximum speed.

*Above* The steeplechase jockey needs far shorter leathers than a show jumper or eventer.

*Opposite* The show jumper needs accurate control to negotiate turns and to lengthen or shorten the pace.

about their horse's ability or lack of ability to stay. As far as position is concerned, all the jockey requires is an exaggerated shortening of the leather, enabling transference of his or her weight to match that of the galloping horse and a 'saddle' that is no more than a pad to which stirrup leathers are attached, thereby reducing weight.

Race riding is an art unto itself. It is only vaguely related to horsemanship as perfected by the classical rider.

## THE REIN AIDS

The use of the leg and the relative importance of this as an aid has been examined. Of equal importance are the hand aids. To be more accurate, we ought to refer to 'hand aids' as 'rein aids'. The function of the hand is primarily to attach the rein to the rider's arm. The rein itself should be held close to the base of the fingers, with the hand naturally curled. It is a popular misconception that a so-called 'light hand' is one in which the rein is held in the fingertips. A simple experiment of holding something with one's fingers as opposed to a naturally curved hand will reveal which position causes tension, leading to insensitivity, and which position gives a soft feel. In relaxation the human hand is slightly curved. Therefore, to provide a soft and sensitive coupling between arm and rein, the hand must be allowed to adopt this relaxed position.

The function of the rein aid will vary among 'allowing', 'denying' and merely 'following'. The movement, or restriction of movement, comes from what can be described as a 'lightly sprung' elbow joint which can be locked in position when required so that the forearm, wrist and hand become merely an extension of the rein. Obviously, the upper arm will move to allow the elbow to function, be it following or allowing, and will also play its part in denying movement in the horse's head and neck when required.

## AN INDEPENDENT SEAT

A horse carrying a rider faces a similar problem to a human carrying a rucksack. If it is not properly fitted, it is able to swing out of position and to move independently of the carrier, it becomes an intolerable burden. Should a walker jump a stream carrying a loosely attached rucksack, their balance may well be lost and the severity of the obstacle thereby increased. So it is for the horse carrying the rider. Insecurity of the jockey, leading to involuntary movement and loss of balance, will destroy the horse's confidence. In extreme cases, this insecurity of position can lead to saddle sores and strain on the horse's back and legs. Where balance is lost, misuse of the rein can lead to bit injuries and insensitivity.

A natural talent to feel the horse's movement and ability to co-ordinate the aids will differ with different riders but sensitivity is essential in the riding and training of horses. A lack of this natural feel can be overcome, to a certain extent, with patient training and guidance, as long as the rider is sensitive and compassionate.

While in every sport there are a favoured few who have exceptional powers of feel, eye, balance or timing and who get to the top through their possession of these priceless gifts, for the vast majority of us, sheer hard work, practice and repetition, coupled with a willingness to learn, have to take the place of natural genius. Our performance can be improved through effort and our sense of achievement satisfied, even though we never ever reach the giddy heights attained by the natural expert.

## SCHOOLING THE YOUNG HORSE

As the horse's athletic ability and obedience improve through basic training, the exercises asked of it can become more demanding. Lungeing should continue, as should transitions from one gait to another in order to develop a fluid balance. Rhythm will develop from this balance. Never allow the horse to become bored or stale. It must have variety in its work as well as progressive and systematic training aimed at developing its ability so that it can tackle what is subsequently asked of it with confidence and keenness.

When training a young horse, I like to run the flatwork alongside the jumping. Of course, the horse must be able to walk, trot and canter on both reins and respect the aids for starting, stopping, accelerating and decelerating before any polework can begin. If one waits until the gaits are nearly perfect before attempting any pole-work, all the newfound balance and rhythm will be lost anyway!

## LATERAL MOVEMENT

Once the horse responds to the aids for forward movement and is receptive to a sympathetic contact from the rider's hand in schooling, hacking out and jumping small obstacles, both indoors and out of doors, lateral work can begin. Repetition of the school movements learnt earlier must still continue, including turn on the forehand and increasing and decreasing the size of your circles. Neither collection nor bend is required in leg-yielding, so this provides an excellent introduction, for both horse and rider, to moving partially sideways. If difficult lateral movements are asked for too soon, the rider will be tempted to 'pull' the horse into shape and will be too forceful with the aids. This will lead to resistance and stiffness through the horse's back, which is detrimental to its training both on the flat and over fences. It is advisable, especially in the early stages of teaching lateral movements, that the horse is equipped with brushing boots all round. The first stages of lateral movement are taught by enlarging the circle through use of the rider's inside leg, as described on p.87.

Equally important, but more difficult, is decreasing the circle size through the use of the rider's outside leg while maintaining a bend in the direction of the movement, i.e. the first steps of half-pass.

In the following paragraphs, 'inside' and 'outside' refer to the inside of the bend, i.e. the shortened side, and, conversely, the outside or lengthened curve of the horse's back. Sometimes 'inside' and 'outside' will coincide with the inside or outside of the school or manège but not always. It is, therefore, important that the terms inside and outside are recognized from the start as referring to the bend of the horse, *not* to its geographic position.

In dressage terms, 'straightness' means that the horse's hind legs are following in the tracks of the forelegs. From this it can be deduced that the horse can be straight even while executing a circular movement. However, when I refer to straightness in the following paragraphs, I do not imply a dressage interpretation. My use of the term 'straight' in this context means that the backbone of the horse is parallel to the side of the manège or, where no manège is available, is at right angles to the general direction of forward movement.

## Leg-yielding

Leg-yielding is the first elementary movement and is therefore the easiest. The horse is asked to move sideways, keeping the body straight but with a small amount of bend at the poll, away from the movement. The steps must be long, smooth and regular, with the inside fore- and hind legs passing in front of the outside fore- and hind legs.

The movement will help to co-ordinate the rider's hand and leg aids and will assist in the acquisition of feel. As far as the horse's education is concerned, it will help to supple its shoulders and back, thereby improving the steps and movement. It also introduces the horse to the meaning of leg aids.

Before the exercise begins, the horse must be round and be moving forward with impulsion. If the horse is bent slightly to the right and is stepping to the left, the rider's right leg is the inside leg. It is this leg that tells the horse to move sideways. The position of the rider's inside leg depends entirely on whether the shoulders or quarters need the control. Remember that the horse must stay straight throughout its body, so the riders' leg must be positioned to achieve this goal. The inside hand asks for a slight bend at the poll. The required degree of bend allows the rider just to glimpse the horse's inside eye but no more. If the cheek and jowl or inner end of the bit in the horse's mouth are visible, the bend is excessive.

The outside rein will control the speed and bend and prevent the horse from escaping through the outside shoulder. The outside hand and leg must operate together to prevent the horse drifting through the outside shoulder by 'closing the door'.

The rider must sit straight and maintain the impulsion through the use of both legs. The arms must remain relaxed and sympathetic

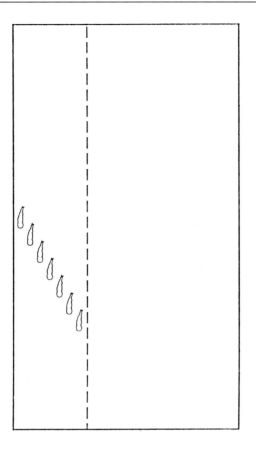

Leg yielding from the
centre line to the track.

and should at no time cross over the horse's neck. The exercise
can be executed by turning down the school three-quarter line
and, using the natural attraction of the school wall or boundary
fence, leg-yielding back to the track. As the horse improves, it can
be asked to go from the centre line back to the track. From there
the movement can be developed across the diagonal. Leg-yield
should be ridden in walk at first before progressing to trot.

## WORKING-IN

Schooling sessions need not be restricted to an arena but can be
included at any time the horse is being ridden. The horse must
become used to being asked to concentrate in different places.
Transitions can easily be perfected while out on a hack and the
horse must not become excited if asked to perform circles in an
open space. Asking the horse to work under different circumstances will not only get it to accept the wishes of the rider at all
times but also provide variation in background and environment
and thereby bring freshness to an often-repeated lesson.

It is difficult to specify the length of time that each schooling
session should take at this stage but, on average, about 30 to 45

minutes should be sufficient. Approximately the first ten minutes should be used to loosen the horse's muscles and eliminate any high spirits. This can be done on the lunge or by being ridden. In either case, start by walking the horse forward in a purposeful medium walk. If the horse is fresh, it is advisable to go on into a working trot as soon as possible. If the horse is on the lunge, the side-reins should be attached after a couple of circles in trot on each rein. I do not ride the horse in with a loose rein as I believe this allows it to work in a hollow shape, while if it is fresh, it also gives it the opportunity to buck! I prefer to spend this warm-up period with a light contact so that the work pattern is established from the beginning of the session.

During this period, large circles should be ridden, with the horse in a good, forward-going stride and even rhythm. Once this has been achieved, the horse can be asked to work a little harder by increasing the severity of the exercises asked.

## TURNS AND CIRCLES

Once the young horse learns to listen to and accept the rider's lateral aids, it is possible to start riding smaller circles and ask more of the horse. The shallow loops that were used during the basic training of the young horse can either be increased in depth or increased in number, i.e. making two loops down the long side of the arena. Small circles, of 10 m (33 ft) in diameter, can be introduced in the corners of the arena; 10-m (33-ft) half circles and returning to the track can be used to change the rein. When the horse can maintain its balance and rhythm on these exercises, it can be asked to make a 10-m figure of eight across the short end of the arena, changing the bend on the centre line. A 10-m (33-ft) figure of eight can also be ridden down the long side of the arena.

## HALF-HALT

It is important that the horse can be shortened or lengthened without any resistance. The horse should have been ridden forward into a sympathetic hand during the early stages of training but it also has to be willing to go down into a lower gear with shorter steps as it progresses. The half-halt is exactly what the name suggests. To ask for a half-halt, the rider uses a combination of leg, weight and hand aids, by sitting in the saddle and closing the legs around the horse, while both hands receive the impulsion and quietly hold. As the horse's weight comes back on to its hocks, the rider allows with the hands and rides the horse forward.

The half-halt can be used to rebalance the horse and prepare it for the next movement. At first, these aids may confuse the horse,

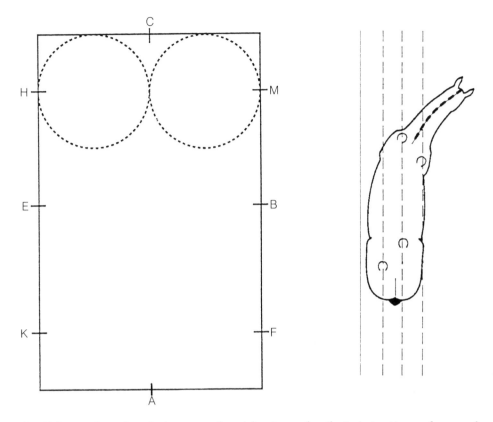

*Left* A 10-m (33-ft) figure of eight across the short end of the arena.

*Right* Shoulder-in.

but it is up to the rider to make their intentions clear and reward the horse when compliance has been achieved.

The halt is a continuation of the half-halt. Once the horse has stopped, the rider must relax the contact. At first, the horse is allowed to make the transition progressive but, as training advances, the transition becomes acute. From the beginning, the horse must halt with its weight evenly distributed on all four legs.

## SHOULDER-IN

Once the horse is happy with the previous exercises and can maintain a rounded shape in balance, shoulder-in can be introduced. This is another exercise in which the horse is bent away from the direction of the movement. It remains bent to either left or right and moves on three tracks down the side of the arena. The horse's hind legs remain on the track and the forehand moves across on to the inside track. The aids given by the rider are similar to those given for a bend. The inside leg operates on the girth in an 'on, push and off' movement; the outside leg holds behind the girth to stop the hindquarters moving outwards. The outside hand allows or denies forward movement, i.e. forward progress, and influences the amount of bend in the neck, while the inside hand asks for direction. At no time should the inside hand become too strong or restrictive or cross over the horse's neck. It may have to be 'played' with in a give and take manner to maintain the bend as, if the aids become fixed and tight, the horse's inside hind leg will become cramped.

In the early stages, shoulder-in should be introduced in walk. When the basic lesson has been learnt, it can be attempted in trot. This can be either sitting or rising trot – always start in rising and then, when the horse's muscles are strong enough, try sitting. If sitting trot is attempted too soon, the horse will hollow its back away from the rider's weight and the hocks will trail out behind, having the opposite effect on the horse to that which is desired. Once it has been decided to include sitting trot in the training, it is essential to use a back pad or numnah under the saddle even if this fits perfectly. Thoroughbred horses have notoriously weak backs and cannot stand the use of strong back aids from the rider in the early stages of training, so they always need some protection.

## CANTER

The majority of schooling work is done in trot but, obviously, canter must also be included. It need not be practised in every session but must be used fairly regularly otherwise the horse will become overexcited whenever it is asked for. The horse must be encouraged to carry itself and canter with a soft contact. If it loses its balance and rhythm, a series of half-halts must be given to restore its equilibrium. The rider must never resort to pulling on the reins, either in an attempt to make the horse go slower or with a shorter stride, because the horse will then pull back and lose the natural spring to its steps. Once the basic canter steps have been spoiled, it is virtually impossible to resurrect them and if the spring has gone it may affect the horse's jumping ability.

In order to counteract the tendency of pupils to use excessively strong rein aids and neglect the aids of leg and back, I was always taught to go forward into a downward transition or halt – even forward into rein-back. Preceding each command with the phrase 'forward into' reminds the rider that downward transitions and halting need the engagement of the horse's hind legs and hocks. To obtain this engagement, it is necessary to use leg and back aids.

Transitions from canter to trot and back to canter again, in quick succession, will teach the horse to activate its hocks and carry itself. Transitions within the gait, from working canter to medium canter to working canter, are also a useful exercise. Particular attention on the part of the instructor should also be paid to downward transitions, as the excitement generated by quick changes of gait can easily lead to overaccentuated hand aids. The horse must be able to increase and decrease its pace without collapsing on to its forehand and therefore throughout the flatwork and, of course, when the horse is being asked to jump a course of fences, the rider's hand must be allowing and maintain a soft contact. Any exercises that combine the requirements of both flatwork and jumping are excellent. One such exercise is to place a pole on the ground in the arena. It is good practice for the horse to canter over this and learn to alter its stride while still maintaining a good balance and rhythm.

In the canter, the horse must be encouraged to bring its inside hind leg well underneath it. Starting the canter on a 20-m (66-ft) circle and spiralling this down to as small a circle as the horse can manage will activate the inside hind leg. Once the horse has cantered a small circle, it must be spiralled back out again on to the 20-m (66-ft) circle. Having got the hind leg well engaged under the horse, the quality of the canter must be maintained for as long as possible. The length of time that this can be achieved will increase as the horse becomes stronger and more able to carry itself.

# USING POLES AND LEARNING TO JUMP

Throughout the training of the young horse, your ultimate goal is to develop its suppleness, agility, rhythm and balance so that it is capable of using its body to the best advantage. Schooling and gymnastic work over poles and small fences will help to achieve this end as well as providing variety in its work.

When using poles on the ground, the distance and spacing between the poles is obviously of importance. However, any distances given in books should only be used as a guide and not rigidly adhered to. Many factors will influence the exact spacing: the size of horse or pony, the state of the going, the levelness of the ground, whether sloping up- or downhill, the speed of approach, the temperament of the animal – all of these can affect the spacing of the poles. Only experience will teach the trainer.

## POLEWORK

Poles can be used either to develop the horse's work on the flat or as an introduction to jumping. Any poles used must be stout and great care must be taken as poles have some disadvantages: they roll easily and they cannot be raised except by the use of blocks or jump stands. The ground must also be flat, with no dips or holes. A sand arena is preferable to grass as the surface will not become either slippery or hard but the going can be deep, so care must be taken not to overwork the young horse and make it tired.

### Flatwork
In flatwork, the use of poles will continue to teach obedience and develop balance and rhythm. Poles will also teach mental and physical co-ordination, calmness and concentration. By lowering

its head and neck to look at the poles, the horse rounds its back and engages its hocks so that the correct muscles will develop. The stride can be regulated and established and, in some cases, lengthened by the use of poles.

At first, the young horse is asked to walk over a single pole with the rider inclining their upper body forward slightly in order not to interfere with the horse's back. After it has become accustomed to going over one pole, another can be added 2.7 m (9 ft) away. (The distances given here apply to horses of approximately 16 h.h.; smaller horses and ponies will require shorter spacings.) The trainer must be precise with the setting of the poles so that confidence can be built up. Putting the poles at this distance allows the horse to walk, trot or canter over them without any fear of treading on them. Because there is plenty of room between them, the horse does not become overawed as it might on the approach to a line of poles. Once the young pupil is walking over

Polework is very good exercise for developing balance and rhythm.

the two poles while maintaining its balance and rhythm and also reaching downwards and forwards with its head and neck, another pole can be added. Up to four or five poles can be put down at an average, but constant, 2.7 m (9 ft) apart (depending on the length of stride).

The horse should be ridden towards the poles in medium walk and, just before the first pole, allowed to go forward and encouraged to lower its neck and lift its back. When it is relaxed and confident about walking over the poles, trot can be introduced. At this stage, the rider must take up rising trot and not sit heavily on the horse's back. Sitting trot must not be adopted until the young is strong enough to carry the rider's weight as this will not encourage it to round its back. It is essential in all this work that the horse is relaxed and obedient, without tension or resistance. At any sign of rushing, it must be circled away and worked on the circle until it is relaxed and obedient again.

When the horse becomes accomplished at trotting over the poles at the open distances, they can be closed to approximately 1.3 m (4 ft 6 in). Four or five poles will be adequate as any more will place too much strain on the horse and become confusing for it. Do not use only two poles at this distance in case the horse is tempted to try to jump over them.

*Opposite* When the horse becomes accomplished at trotting over the poles at 2.7 m (9 ft), they can be closed up to 1.3 m (4 ft 6 in) apart.

*Below* Placing the poles 2.7 m (9 ft) apart gives the horse plenty of room between each pole.

All work performed over poles must be carried out with the horse in a round shape and maintaining a good rhythm. The rider must be spontaneous and lavish with praise and reward when the work is completed well.

When using poles, *never* walk over them when spaced 1.3 m (4 ft 6 in) apart as this is the wrong distance for the walk stride and will only upset a young horse.

## Exercises

Work over the poles must never be hurried but a good rhythm should be developed. The poles can be placed in a straight line down the edge of the arena, across the diagonal or in a fan-shape, following the line of a circle. Obviously, patterns that are set out in other than a straight line pose more of a problem to the horse as it has to maintain its rhythm and impulsion on the corners and execute a smooth, flowing turn. Poles on a circle can help to make the horse more supple. Just as in its flatwork on a circle, the horse has to shorten the distance between its head and haunches on the inside, while extending a similar amount on the outside to follow the circumference of the circle or the arc of a bend. The inside hind leg will carry more weight and must come further underneath the horse's body. The length of the stride can be altered by increasing or decreasing the radius of the curved track to be followed.

Different positions for trotting poles.

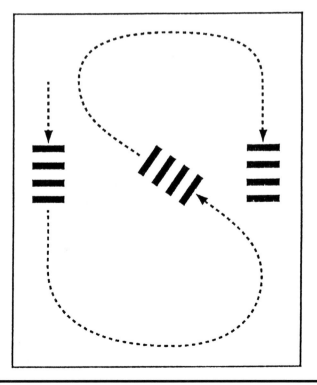

The poles can also be placed on the centre line of the arena. This will ensure that a correct corner and turn are ridden, so that the horse arrives at the centre of the first pole in balance, straight and in a good rhythm.

The horse must not proceed any further in its training until it can perform over the trotting poles confidently and in a relaxed manner. If any problems are experienced, the trainer must be prepared to return to walking over a single pole or trotting over the more open, 2.7-m (9-ft) spaced poles. Poles raised off the ground put a tremendous strain on young horses and, if used, great care must be exercised. Conventional, knife-rest cavaletti should should be used on the lowest register and never turned to increase the height. At this increased height, their only permissible use is to provide simple and adjustable heights of jumps. For walking or trotting, the cardinal rule is as low to the ground as possible.

## JUMPING

In its natural environment the wild horse had no need to jump. A creature of the plains and prairies, it met no obstructions other than streams and ditches to impede its progress. There was little necessity to add height to width when traversing such obstacles and little more than lengthening of the stride was necessary. Comparatively recently, the Enclosures Act in Britain, and similar legislation abroad, resulted in hedges and fences appearing across the countryside. Initially, it was the owner of the horse used for hunting who found it necessary to teach his mount to add height to width in order to cross the country. Hunting then developed a sideline called point-to-pointing, the forerunner of racing over obstacles. As the name implies, a point-to-point was a race from point A to point B. These 'points' were often the steeples of churches, thus giving rise to the modern term 'steeplechase'. A further development was the more sophisticated test of a horse's ability in the show ring to jump over artificial obstacles – show jumping.

It can be seen, therefore, that the horse's ability to jump was not a natural progression in its evolution. As it is a requirement imposed by people, it is therefore necessary for people to teach the horse to do it.

No horse can be made to jump well by using force. Jump training is best started from trot so that the young horse is discouraged from rushing. It also means that it will have time to look at the fence, judge its point to take-off and also arrive at that point with two legs on the ground. Having established rhythm, balance and co-ordination over the line of trotting poles, a small cross pole (of approximately 60 cm or 2 ft where the poles cross) can be added 2.7 m (9 ft) after the final trotting pole. This must be approached in trot. If at any time the horse becomes anxious and attempts to rush through the poles, it must be circled away and relaxed. The rider must never check on the reins within the last stride to the poles, as the horse cannot make late adjustments. Its eyes are set on the sides of its head, making its focus point some 2.7 m (9 ft) in front of it, so by then all arrangements will already have been made to negotiate the obstacle in front of it and the last stride is 'blind'.

The basic idea of three or four trotting poles followed by a cross pole can be developed in a variety of different patterns. It can be made into an easy spread fence by adding a horizontal pole directly behind the cross, making the width approximately 30–60 cm (1–2 ft). Another cross pole can then be added 5.5 m (18 ft) from the first. This fence can also be made into a spread as the confidence of the horse develops. A distance of 5.5 m will enable the horse to take one non-jumping stride between the two elements. The second element can be widened and raised until it eventually becomes a parallel. Always keep the first fence small and inviting. If things are going smoothly, you can dispense with the trotting poles and use only a placing pole, laid on the ground 2.7 m (9 ft) from the first jump.

*Below* Once the horse is working well over the poles, a small fence can be added.

*Above* Schooling a horse loose over small fences will help to develop its self-confidence.

## Loose Schooling over Jumps

Earlier in its training, it is possible that the young horse will have been loose schooled. This can now be continued and, at this stage, can include some fences. Every fence must be well constructed and inviting for the horse and have a substantial wing. Trotting poles or a placing pole should not be used in loose jumping. The same rules as for loose schooling on the flat will apply but, in addition, it is important that the horse must never be overfaced by too demanding a fence.

I would recommend that a small cross-pole fence is built 5.5 m (18 ft) in front of a small spread fence. As the horse progresses, this second fence can be made higher and wider. During each session, these fences should not be jumped more than six or seven times and the session should always finish over a small obstacle so that the horse returns to its stable happy and relaxed.

## Jumping with a Rider

Frequent changes in the direction of approach to the fence should be made. In the early stages, jumping towards home, i.e. the stable, will often encourage the novice. This must not be overdone, however, or the stage may be reached at which the horse anticipates the excitement of jumping and starts to rush its fences.

When the horse is trotting quietly into upright and spread cross-poles, the fence can be changed. The poles on the upright can be laid across horizontally, with one pole remaining on the ground as a groundline and also with a placing pole 2.7 m (9 ft) before the fence. When first altering the spread fence, the front part should remain crossed with only the back pole horizontal, so that it encourages the horse to jump in the middle of the fence and to keep straight. These fences should be approached in working trot with the rider rising. As the horse's confidence grows, it may be allowed to canter the last couple of strides. Keep your placing pole at 2.7 m (9 ft).

As the horse progresses to jumping combinations, I find it best to use one non-jumping stride between the elements. The distance will be approximately 5.5 m (18 ft) from trot, progressing to 6.4 m (21 ft) for canter and 7.3 m (24 ft) for canter when the fences become higher or wider. The use of one non-jumping stride is not universally adopted when teaching a youngster to jump and there is a body of opinion that advocates two non-jumping strides when introducing doubles. However, with two strides the horse is inclined to flatten and transfer its weight on to its forehand. When the horse is happily negotiating a one non-jumping stride double, it can be introduced to a two non-jumping stride combination, approximately 10.3 m (34 ft) to 11 m (36 ft) apart.

## Building Schooling Fences

Great care must always be taken when building fences of any kind but especially when erecting obstacles in order to teach young horses how to jump.

A horse will measure the jump from the groundline upwards and judges where to take off from that point. For this reason, the bottom of the fence needs to be solid and clearly defined. A pole lying on the ground slightly in front of an upright fence will act as a good groundline and help the horse to take off from the correct point. Always remember that poles on the ground should be securely pegged. A rolling pole can cause a serious accident should the horse tread on it and, in any case, will reduce the confidence of the young jumper, who needs reassurance above all at this stage. Fences that slope away from the point of take-off are the most inviting for a horse to negotiate. This follows the natural shape of the horse's jump and is therefore comparatively easy for the horse to traverse. Except in Puissance, the horse will always be asked to jump on the smooth arc of the circle and this also fits the profile of a fence sloping away from the take-off. Conversely, to reverse the profile of the jump, making it concave from the approach, will greatly increase the severity of the obstacle. Removal of the groundline, which provides the point from which the horse measures its take-off, combined with a concave face towards the approach line, could render the obstacle, if not impossible, then extremely difficult to negotiate.

If the groundline of the fence is directly underneath the front pole or set back behind the vertical, this will confuse the horse and cause it to get too close for take-off. This type of fence should not be used with the novice horse.

The correct point for take-off will depend on the height and shape of the fence, the terrain and the type of ground surface. Over vertical fences up to approximately 1.2 m (4 ft), the take-off zone would be a distance from the base of the fence that is roughly one and a half times the height of the fence. This is approximately the centre of the take-off zone, which is the most advantageous place for the horse to take off to negotiate the fence. The larger the fence, the more important it is to get in deeper to the base. True parallels should be jumped in a similar manner to a vertical fence. A sloping fence or staircase profile encourages the horse to stand off by as much as the height of the fence and will match the parabola of its flight.

## TYPES OF FENCE

### The Ascending Staircase or Sloping Parallel

Fences that slope away from the point of take-off are most inviting for the horse to jump.

This can take the form of a cross-pole with a horizontal element behind it to make a simple spread. A triple bar or ascending parallel, in which the back pole is higher than the front, will constitute a more easily negotiable spread fence.

## A Hogsback

This type of obstacle is also very straightforward as it slopes away from the point of take-off. Basically, this obstacle provides a sloping approach and a sloping departure. It therefore matches the natural flight of the horse through the air. It can be a comparatively impressive fence as a result of its dimensions but is technically a simple fence within the restrictions of the horse's general ability. A tiger-trap is a jump where there are sloping poles over a ditch in the ground. This type of fence can be approached from either side and is relatively easy to jump. It will also encourage the horse to bascule (round its back) over the fence as it looks down to see what is on the landing side.

## Upright Fences

An upright fence is exactly what the name implies. It is any type of jump that is vertical and has no width, for example, a gate, a set of planks or just poles set in a vertical plane. These are all difficult to jump as the horse and rider have to arrive at the correct point for take-off in order to clear them. The severity of the upright fence

*Above* An upright fence is exactly what the name implies.

will be increased by the emphasis on, or lack of, a groundline. The easiest fence in a vertical plane is one that terminates in a pole on the ground. The most difficult vertical fence is a single pole suspended in mid-air with nothing underneath it. It is the course builder's option to include or preclude a groundline or give a well-filled base to the fence and would depend on the severity of the competition for which the course is being built. Although sometimes employed in cross-country courses, it is seldom acceptable that false groundlines are included in show jumping fences. Cross-country seeks to reproduce natural obstacles such as hedges and ditches and therefore rails or banks may create a false groundline. Such an obstacle can be acceptable in this discipline. In show jumping it is seldom, if ever, tolerated.

### A True Parallel

A true parallel is where the front pole is exactly the same height from the ground as the rear pole. On the approach, it is probable that the horse can only see the first pole. This can cause problems.

In addition, in order to create the parabola of the jump, the horse must visualize an imaginary pole in the centre of the two existing poles but at an additional height. It is this imaginary pole that the horse must negotiate in order to avoid contact with the actual obstacle.

*Below* In a true parallel the front pole is exactly the same height as the rear pole.

## AVOIDANCE OF POSSIBLE FUTURE PROBLEMS

The horse should now be accustomed to being hacked out in the company of another horse. Hillwork can be included in the sessions to improve its suppleness and ability to balance and help itself. When riding uphill, the rider must incline their body slightly forward to transfer the weight off the seatbones on to the fork, thighs and knees. This gives more freedom to the horse's loins and hindquarters to act as the powerhouse to ascend gradients.

When coming downhill, it is vital that the horse is kept straight. If the horse is allowed to go down at an angle, it may possibly lose its balance and fall. Going downhill, the rider should incline the body slightly forward, except if the slope has a steeper angle than 60 degrees, where it will be necessary to lean slightly back. The rider must always keep a light contact on the reins, remembering that the head and neck act as a balancing pole for the horse and therefore the freedom of the head must not be interfered with. It is always better to hold on to a piece of mane or the front arch of the saddle or a martingale strap while going either up- or downhill, rather than catching balance on the reins.

Riding out across country can teach the young horse how to cope with all sorts of different terrain, including going up and down hills. Natural obstacles can also be included, providing they are safe and small. Ditches are probably the most frequently encountered obstacles. Young horses must be encouraged to jump as many as possible, following an escort in the beginning stages until their confidence grows. It is the depth of this unusual obstacle that normally concerns the horse, not the actual width.

Find a shallow, dry ditch and approach it at walk. It is always advisable to have a neckstrap to tuck the fingers into because, especially in the case of a young horse, the horse can suddenly make an exaggerated jump. If there is no lead horse available, the horse must be allowed to investigate the obstacle by standing at the edge and lowering its head and neck to have a look. This is the moment of truth! Be prepared for a sudden leap as confidence flows into your mount and it leaps five times the size of the obstacle, leaving you clutching its tail. While allowing the horse ample opportunity for reconnaissance, you should have already tucked your fingers into the mane, front arch of the saddle or neckstrap, ready for the unpredictable leap. While anticipating this movement, make certain that your weight is slightly forward of the perpendicular otherwise you may well still find yourself getting left behind.

As soon as the horse is confident when following a companion, it must learn to go on its own. Provided progression has been made in undemanding steps over a period of time, the confidence should be there to allow the pupil to attempt obstacles on its own. If problems of lack of confidence occur, leading to refusals, there should be no hestitation in returning to the confident example of a lead horse. When the horse has learnt to make its own way and is obedient to the aids, ditches can be approached in canter and can even have water in the bottom.

Whenever it rains heavily, resulting in the flooding of roadways, paths or ditches, water training can be introduced. Again, it is advisable to use a lead horse. The more experienced horse can walk through the water, followed by the inexperienced one. When this is accomplished, trot can be introduced. A dry ditch that has already been negotiated by the young horse will not appear as terrifying an obstacle when flooded as a strange water-filled ditch. It cannot be overstressed that, when teaching a young horse to negotiate water, its confidence must not be undermined by doubts concerning the soundness of the footing under the water. This is even more important when jumping into or out of water is concerned. The trainer must always test the going before using any water obstacles and the only way to do this is to wade through on foot oneself. One traumatic experience in water for a young horse can make it a 'stopper' for life when faced with a water jump. If there is a safe flood, such as a minor road ford, both horses can be made to stand or walk around in it so that their confidence is built up.

If the ultimate object of the trainer is to produce a show jumper, all emphasis in its training regarding water obstacles will be to achieve a clear jump over water. If, however, the ultimate object is to produce an eventer, the horse must be taught to jump clear over water or into and out of water, according to the instructions of its rider. It is obvious which result requires the greater skill on the part of the trainer and greater ability on the part of the horse. To teach the horse to jump over water, it is necessary for the rider to understand that, provided the height of the jump is obtained, the width will automatically follow. For example, to clear 3.6 m (12 ft) of open water, it is necessary to jump approximately 1.2 m (4 ft) high over the centre of the spread. Talking in general terms, a horse will take off roughly one and a half times the height of the fence from the base of the fence. It will then land approximately one and a half times the height of the fence away from the obstacle. Even without a computer, it is possible to see that a 1.2-m (4-ft) high jump over a spread of 3.6 m (12 ft) at ground level will be successful.

With these facts in mind, the trainer should place a pole, possibly filled in underneath, approximately 1.06  m − 1.14 m (3 ft 6 in − 3 ft 9 in) over the water at a distance of about 1.06  m from take-off. The take-off line on the leading edge of the water

should be clearly defined by a small brush fence or logs. The effect of this should be to lift the horse over the spread. As training progresses, so the aids for height inducement and, eventually, take-off accentuation, can be reduced, until the horse is confident about facing and clearing an open stretch of water. This should provide a sound base for water-jump negotiation in the future.

With both show jumpers and event horses, it is necessary to acquire an ability to jump obstacles that are combined with water. This will obviously necessitate careful training.

The simplest method is to utilize an obstacle in your training area that comprises a permanent ditch of reasonable width, i.e. approximately 90 cm (3 ft), with a movable brush fence or something of similar 'non-see-through' character that is longer than the ditch.

To start with, the horse should be circled on a wide arc on its favourite cantering leg. The fence should be on the take-off side of the water ditch, at about 90 cm (3 ft) or 99 cm (3 ft 3 in) high. The horse, not seeing the ditch behind it, will happily negotiate the obstacle. The exercise should be repeated several times on the same rein and with the same approach. Gradually, the fence should be moved back, approximately 15 cm (6 in) at a time, to reveal more of the ditch in front of the fence, but only after a few reassuring jumps with it in its original position. Before going too far on the favourite leg, the whole exercise should be repeated from square one on the less favourable rein. Through succeeding training sessions on each rein, the width of the water in front of the jump can be increased. Ultimately, more 'see-through' fences can be substituted, such as rails on both take-off and landing sides. The speed of progression will be determined by the confidence of the individual horse. Never overtake that confidence and overface the pupil.

The event horse must be schooled to enter water with or without a fence, according to its rider's wishes. The first essential is to eliminate fear of water from the mind of the pupil, at the same time retaining respect for the qualities of water. If there is a large puddle in the field that has not caused serious deterioration of the going, the first experience of jumping into water can start. This is not a very wise exercise on heavy clay land but is possible in light soils.

Always start by walking through the water and then progressing to trot. The next stage is to trot over a pole on the ground (suitably secured) or a small log, using the same direction of approach. Be wary of raising the initial jump too quickly and vary the direction of approach from time to time. With larger fences, the quality of the going underwater becomes far more important as the penetration of the horse's feet will become greater the

Riding out will help to build the young horse's confidence.

higher it jumps. So, other than for use with an elementary pole on the ground, flood puddles in fields must now be abandoned in favour of specially constructed, hard-bottomed water obstacles with a covering of sand or pea gravel over the hardcore base. Sometimes a small, quiet, soft-bedded (i.e. not tarmac) country lane with a ford can be used (with an assistant and an easily movable obstacle in case traffic should come by), while some river beds will give the opportunity to practise jumping off the bank with or without the obstacle included. Always check the underwater going by walking through yourself on foot. This should be done before *every* session.

Should a trainer decide to construct a water obstacle, be it an over, into or through jump, for the first time, the advice of an experienced course builder should be sought.

Anyone who has waded through water is aware of the drag or resistance set up by the water. The deeper it is, the stronger the resistance. For this reason, the young horse must always be introduced to water obstacles of little depth. As the horse's confidence and agility grow, so the depth of the water can gradually be increased. Those wading through water, be they human, equine or canine, will find that to push a leg through deeper water not only requires greater effort but also interferes with balance as the upper body tends to outstrip the forward progress of the legs, which can result in total immersion! If you think of a bather running down the beach and into the sea you will realize that the deeper the water gets, the higher the knees must be raised to reduce the drag of the water and the risk of toppling forwards. Similarly, a dog, though it can canter into shallow fringes of water, will drop back to a trot as the depth increases. Follow these examples when training a horse. Never canter through water of any significant depth; always trot.

Some people take their horses hunting in order to introduce them to jumping unfamiliar obstacles and to learn to jump in the company of others. Personally, I believe that, nowadays, young horses that show any potential are too valuable to risk in the hunting field. In any case, modern farming techniques in the UK have created large areas of arable land which does not lend itself to hunting as readily as it did in the days when fields were small and grass more prevalent. Efficient farms are far more like efficient factories than a way of living and many farmers do not welcome inexperienced young horses crashing through their fences and gates.

An alternative to hunting is hunter trialling. The courses are mostly over natural obstacles and will form an introduction to the cross country phase of a one day event. Hunter trials are held in the spring and autumn and should be ridden at a steady canter. Use them as a training exercise and do not be tempted to gallop for the

Hunter trials provide a good introduction to the cross-country phase of a one day event.

fastest time. Most hunter trials will have a pairs class, which is ideal for the inexperienced horse who may need a lead over an unusual obstacle. In addition, many cross-country courses can be hired for a schooling practice.

You must continue with gymnastic exercises and jumping fences at related distances. Grids teach the horse to be agile in body as well as in mind and to jump in rhythm and balance. The horse must learn to look after itself when necessary. However accomplished the rider, mistakes and miscalculations will occur from time to time and a horse that is capable of taking appropriate action to save the situation of its own volition will be a very great asset, especially when going round a cross-country course.

In addition to 'normal' jumping obstacles, i.e. uprights, parallels (true or ascending) or sloping spreads, specialized cross-country fences should also include ditches in front of or behind an obstacle, ditches without an obstacle, graded banks to provide drops of varying severity, on and off platforms and slides with a small obstacle at the top. These types of fences may be used as a single fence, either free-standing as an island or in a natural or artificial fence line, or in combination with one or more differing elements. Into this latter category will come such fences as small sheep pens, farm yards, etc. and coffins comprising three obstacles, usually an upright, ditch and upright at related distances. The coffin can prove to be one of the most difficult jumps in a course, especially if the horse can see through the first element to the ditch beyond.

With all these cross-country obstacles, the terrain will have great effect upon their severity. It can often be considered a luxury to meet a fence on a level site. It is therefore essential for the young horse to be trained to jump uphill, downhill and across the gradient if it is to make an eventer.

Practice cross-country fences should be solidly built. They should neither knock down nor break if hit. It is essential that the young horse respects cross-country fences and does not expect them to disintegrate in the same way a show jump does. It is a mistaken idea that knock-down fences should be used in the initial stages of training. Not only does this practice lead to the wrong lessons being taught but it can also prove to be a hazard to the safety of horse and rider. Poles that fly and become entangled in front legs, poles that roll downhill when dislodged and trip up the horse, poles that splinter into sharp projections are all highly dangerous.

After the young horse has been introduced to different types of fences and has learnt to negotiate individual and combination obstacles in an even rhythm and with confidence, it is ready to jump a simple show jumping or cross-country course.

## SHOW JUMPING

The same points that apply to building schooling fences will apply to fences that form part of a course. The fences must be suitably built for the novice horse as outlined on pp. 112–15. Distances between elements in combinations can be made easy and straightforward to suit a stride, or difficult and devious to confound a stride. For the purposes of training, obviously, all combinations should be in the first category. It is debatable whether the second option should ever be used, except possibly at the very highest level for the most experienced horses and riders. For the small horse or pony, a shorter distance between the elements of a

The terrain has a great effect upon the severity of all cross-country obstacles.

combination will be easier and more inviting. Conversely, a larger animal will welcome the extra space of a slightly longer distance.

Riding-in before a round of jumping is of great importance. During this time, the horse will need to do some suppling exercises to loosen it up. It must also be made obedient by doing some transitions. Before attempting the course, a spread and an upright practice fence must be jumped. All horses are different and all will need different amounts of work before reaching their particular best. Be careful not to jump too many times – generally, between three and six fences should be enough.

## Jumping a Course

It is of great importance that the first few courses a young horse is asked to jump are easy and inviting. The person riding the young horse over its first few courses also has an enormous responsibility in the way in which the horse is presented to the fences. It must be turned smoothly and given enough time to see the fence that it is approaching. It must arrive at the centre of each fence so that the line of approach is at right angles to the middle part of the jump. In the early days of jumping a course, the object of the exercise is to teach the horse to jump several fences in balance. The rider must have the horse between the hand and leg after each jump. Should this balance be lost or the horse show a tendency to rush, a large, 'soothing' circle should be completed before attempting the next obstacle. Young horses may start to go faster the further round the course they go, as they lose their balance, becoming excited and making careless mistakes. When jumping a practice course, care must be taken to achieve a calm, steady round without using too forceful aids from hand, back or leg as these will only exacerbate the problem and increase the disobedience of the horse. If the horse does become strong, never be afraid to take a step back and correct the problem by trotting in to fences again or by doing some gymnastic work rather than resorting to a stronger bit or a fashionable gadget.

Jumping will complement the horse's flatwork to a certain extent, first, by loosening the muscles, especially in the back, and, second, by teaching the horse to create its own impulsion and not rely on the rider to produce it. A fence will give a reason for the impulsion to be created; flatwork does not always do this. The same rules will apply over fences as in training the horse on the flat. The horse must be kept calm so that it can use itself to its fullest extent. As with the flatwork, balance and rhythm are of the utmost importance.

Some of the most talented jump riders are born with the gift of being 'able to see a stride' 99 per cent of the time but the vast majority of us are not so blessed! This is one of the main reasons for maintaining a steady rhythm between the fences. If the horse can anticipate where it will meet the obstacle, it can start to make its own arrangements to complete the task confronting it.

The horse must not be chased into fences and only a stronger leg aid or a tap with a stick should be used if the horse seems likely to refuse. In the case of a potential run-out, a tap down the base of the neck may be sufficient to discourage the disobedience. It is, of course, essential to know your horse and to carry your stick in the hand towards which it is most likely to swerve or swing out on a circle. The effect of a strong reprimand will be for the horse to go faster and flatter over the fence; it will not make the horse jump higher nor use itself in a proper shape – correct training is the only answer for this.

Some young horses will need strong riding in the early stages when faced with unusual or difficult fences but as they gain in confidence they must learn to respond to just a squeeze from the leg in order to jump correctly. Correction on the part of the rider must always be administered coolly and quietly, never in anger.

The contact that the rider has with the horse's mouth becomes more important over fences than it was on the flat. The horse must be given total freedom of movement over the fence but the contact must not be cut by simply throwing the reins at it. Imagine yourself holding on to a rope, perhaps even using it in order to keep your balance, and then it breaks. The result will be complete loss of balance, causing you to fall forwards or backwards. The same can happen to the horse, especially if it is taking a strong hold on the rein going in to the fence and, suddenly, the support has gone. All its weight will fall forward and it will land on its forehand, out of balance. Furthermore, the action of throwing the hand forward will also cause the rider to transfer their weight forwards and lose balance.

The perfect contact is light (about the weight of the rein) on the approach. At the point of take-off, the hand and forearm must follow the movement of the horse's head and neck, still maintaining a light contact on the bit as if the rider's elbow was lightly sprung. As the horse stretches and lowers its head and neck, so the rider's arm follows the movement downwards and forwards. The horse will then raise its head and shorten its neck, the 'spring in the elbow' reasserts itself and the rider's hand and arm maintain the contact. The horse will then require to lengthen its neck and lower its head as it bascules over the top of the jump. Again, the hand and arm must follow the movement. On landing, the neck will shorten once again, the head will come up slightly and the spring will reassert itself. This will encourage the horse to lower its head and soften its back so that its hind legs can come underneath it in preparation for the take-off.

Obviously, there are many horses on which the perfect contact will not be possible but the rider must never adopt a dead pull. This will only encourage the horse to lean on the bit and go faster. If there is restriction at the point of take-off, the horse will jump with its head up, its back hollow and trailing its hind legs, which will result in the fence being knocked down. If the horse suffers pain in either limbs or mouth as a result of jumping, its enthusiasm for such activities will be greatly reduced. The importance of remaining calm and forward-thinking in a balanced, rhythmical way cannot be overemphasized enough for both flatwork and jumping.

When a problem arises, its cause must be established first before a successful cure can be attempted. Flatwork will teach the horse to be obedient to the aids and work in a balanced, rhythmical manner. Jumping will help the horse to use its back correctly by stretching the muscles along its topline and will therefore also help its flatwork. In this way, the two disciplines complement each other.

A young horse looking relaxed and happy when jumping.

# NEW EXPERIENCES FOR THE YOUNG HORSE

Part of the training of the young horse is to familiarize it with as many new experiences as possible. These will vary between things encountered outside the stable yard and those within the yard. The more obvious external situations that may lead to problems are traffic, workmen in holes in the road, pneumatic drills, airbrakes and even children on skateboards! In a rural setting, farm machinery can be very frightening to horses, as can stock of various kinds, from guinea fowl via pigs to gadding cattle. The pigeon scarer does not only scare pigeons! While it is obvious that horses used by the police or by the army for ceremonial duty have to be trained to be oblivious of crowds, many an event horse has met its Waterloo because of the crowds of spectators surrounding problem fences.

Within the stable yard many new elements of education will be encountered, some of which may, in the early stages, be upsetting for the young horse. Very early in its training the youngster must learn to be plaited. This will be more important for the competition or show horse than for the hack, although even in this less glamorous category there are occasions when a 'gala performance' is required!

## PLAITING

The mane is normally plaited on the offside (the right-hand side) of the neck. The number of plaits will vary according to the length of the horse's neck and the length of the mane but there should be an uneven number down the neck, excluding the forelock. If the horse has a short neck, a greater number of plaits will help it to appear longer, while the appearance of a long neck can be improved by fewer, fatter plaits. A neck that is lacking in muscle along the topline can also be improved by making the plaits small and round and setting them along the top of the crest. This will carry the observer's eye to the line formed by the plaits not the line of the neck.

The horse must never learn to associate the act of being plaited with something exciting being about to happen. The mane can be plaited to lay it over to one side, in preparation for clipping or just for an ordinary day's work at home. Horses that become agitated or nervous or will not eat once they are plaited, put themselves and their owners under unnecessary stress.

## CLIPPING

Clipping is an essential part of any working horse's education. It is necessary to enable the horse to work hard without sweating, which can cause loss of condition or chills because a heavy coat holds the sweat. It will also assist the groom to keep the horse clean as grooming brushes penetrate a short coat more easily and efficiently than a long coat. There are different types of clip to suit the kind of work the horse is doing, the lifestyle of the horse and the stabling facilities available. If the horse is clipped out completely, the availability of stabling by night and day will be necessary. Partial clipping, such as a trace or blanket clip, is a useful compromise for a horse that cannot be fully stabled.

The normal season for clipping starts in October and continues through into January. It is generally necessary to clip every two to three weeks. It is now becoming increasingly more common for competition horses, especially show jumpers and event horses, to be clipped during the hot summer months. Not only does this reduce the amount of sweating, it also makes it easier to keep the horse clean and smart. When the summer coat is clipped, it does not change in colour like the winter coat but just makes the existing coat thinner. Whenever a horse is completely clipped, it must be stabled, at least at night, and should wear enough rugs to keep it warm. The warmer the horse is kept, the less often it will require clipping.

Always choose a safe, quiet stable that has good natural light and a power point. A circuit breaker should also be used.

The bedding should be partially swept back leaving only a light covering to prevent slipping. Remove any water buckets or feed bowls that may get in the way. Both the person clipping and the assistant must be sensibly dressed. Overalls fastened at the neck will protect clothing and prevent some of the horse's hair from slipping down inside shirts or pullovers to cause irritation. Rubber footwear is absolutely essential whenever electricity is involved.

A well-plaited mane.

Always begin clipping in the morning when the light is best, and allow plenty of time. Providing that they have not had a bad experience when being clipped, most horses enjoy it as much as they enjoy being groomed. When first clipping a young horse, spend a few moments getting it accustomed to the noise of the clipping machine. Ask an assistant to hold the horse and talk to it while the machine is switched on in the doorway. Then show the horse the machine with it turned *off* and let it sniff at it. Keep talking and stroking the horse and do not frighten it with the cable. If it is unconcerned, clipping can begin. Decide the type of clip before commencing and any areas that are to be left should be clearly outlined using chalk, white shoe cleaner or lipstick.

Keep the blades flat and make long strokes against the lay of the coat, starting in the region of the shoulder. Keep the machine well oiled so that the blades do not become too hot. If they do, either change them or take a rest for 15 minutes! Horses are sensitive on their heads, under their bellies and around their stifles and elbows. The blades must be cool for these areas. An assistant will also be required to lift each front leg forward so that the skin around the elbow is pulled tight to prevent cuts. Using small, quiet dog clippers for these awkward areas and the head can make the job a lot easier.

When the clipping is finished, the horse must be groomed, rugged up and put back in its stable. The equipment must then be thoroughly cleaned before being put away.

Hunter clip

High trace
clip

Blanket clip

Medium trace
clip

It cannot be stressed too much how important the first few clips can be for the horse's future life. The asset of having a horse that will stand quietly, indeed, may even appear to enjoy the sensation, is priceless. A horse that has been frightened, roughly handled or even injured during its introduction to clipping will be a danger to itself and its handlers throughout its life when clipping time comes round. This may lead to clipping being done less frequently than is necessary for the health and well-being of the horse. It will certainly lead to a great waste of time and may cause extra expense should sedation become necessary.

## SHOEING

Like clipping, shoeing is an experience where careful, quiet and calm introduction will pay dividends for years to come. Rough handling, overparing, nail-binding or pricking will cause apprehension throughout the horse's life whenever a farrier approaches. Always inform the farrier that he is coming to shoe a young horse for the first time so that he allows sufficient time and does not hurry on to another job. It would be worth while to pay a bit extra on the first few occasions to ensure a trouble-free future.

## 'PARTY GOING'

The young horse should go out to 'parties' several times before it is asked to compete at one. It will need to be introduced to the atmosphere of the strange show ground, a lot of strange horses, flags, loudspeakers and crowds. All this will have a very exciting effect. If the horse was shown in hand as a foal and/or yearling and two-year-old, it will become accustomed to everything much quicker than a horse that has been left in a field and broken at four years old.

### Travelling

The first major experience to overcome is a journey in the horsebox or trailer. During its handling and training, time should have been taken to accustom the horse to the wearing of rugs, bandages and/or boots in preparation for travelling. The horse must be at ease and comfortable and able to walk around in them without kicking or high-stepping. The horse should have been led in and out of the transport and taken for short journeys from a very young age to get it accustomed to travelling. Unfortunately, some horses do not receive this early training and can lead to unnecessary complications even before the day has begun!

Plenty of time must be left for everything that is done with the young horse. If it is at all possible, another, more experienced, sensible horse should be taken along with the young one. When loading, first park the transport on flat ground, so that the ramp is not too steep, and also alongside a wall so that there is a 'wing' on one side of the ramp. Have both horses ready and load the schoolmaster first. Tie it up, adjust the partitions, etc. and then load the youngster. Walk straight forward and with purpose – do not look back. A second person must stand on the open side of the ramp to encourage the horse to walk straight in. You should *never* attempt to load a young horse without an assistant. If difficulty is experienced, two extra helpers will be required. A lunge rein should then be fastened to each side of the vehicle and the two helpers should each hold the free end of one rein. They then cross these over behind the horse so that it cannot pull back as it nears the ramp.

Loading a horse using two lunge reins crossed just above the hocks will prevent it running back.

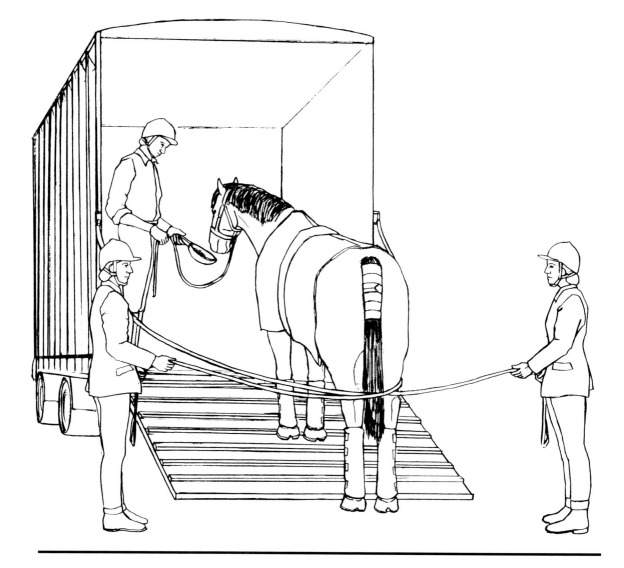

Time must be taken to educate the horse about loading so that it does not become frightened. If the young horse has not been loaded and travelled as a baby, this exercise should be practised before the day of the show. If the preparation has been correct, the loading sequence should not take too long. If the trailer or horsebox has a forward ramp, in addition to the rear ramp, it is a useful exercise to lead the horse up one ramp and down the other to accustom it to the noise and the change in the light. Subsequently, the horse can be led into a stall in the box or trailer, the ramps shut and a feed given as a reward.

Leave plenty of time for the journey. Whenever horses are travelled by road, tremendous care must be taken with the driving. Lorries are generally more stable than trailers so, on a motorway or similar quality road, they can go faster. Both forms of transport must slow down considerably for corners and roundabouts. One bad journey, simply because time is running out, may result in frightening the horse and many hours will then have to be spent in attempting to regain its confidence. There is, of course, no guarantee that this will be successful. It is far better to arrive at the show half an hour early than to arrive in a rush with an upset horse.

On arrival, the ramp of the horse box should be lowered provided there are suitable gates at the top to prevent the horses from coming down while they are still tied up. This will enable them to look out and see what is going on as well as introducing some fresh air to circulate in the back.

In the case of a trailer, it is best to leave the ramp up so that the horses are not tempted to pull back against the breeching straps. If there is a front unload on the trailer the top half may be undone if both horses are relaxed. In either case, it must be appreciated that, with ramps open at each end of the trailer or box, a 'wind tunnel' effect can be created. While this can be an advantage on a hot summer's day, it can be a serious disadvantage in cold weather, especially with an excited and sweating young horse.

When the time comes for the experienced horse to compete, saddle both of them and take them out of the box together.

A period on the lunge can be of benefit to all young horses at shows. It will enable them to release any high spirits and have a look at their exciting new surroundings and will also give an opportunity for their companion to slip away unnoticed. The procedure of the lungeing must be exactly the same as practised at home – a short period in which to loosen up and have time to assess the surroundings, then the side reins are attached and the serious work begins. As at home, the horse must be obedient. After approximately 20 minutes, the horse should be mounted.

It can then be hacked around so that it can quietly absorb the atmosphere of the competition. When it has settled down, a quiet corner must be found where the youngster can be asked to concentrate and do some serious work. The easiest way to do this is to occupy its mind by giving it exercises such as circles, changes of direction and transitions so that it starts to concentrate on what the rider is asking rather than on its own ideas. The rider's voice can be invaluable at this stage as it can be authoritative, calming or encouraging and is never more helpful than in a moment of crisis!

When the collecting ring becomes less crowded, the young horse can be asked to jump a small practice fence. Never ask it to do as much as it can manage at home and always make sure that it has enough room for both the approach to and departure from the fence.

Attention must also be paid to the safety of the practice fence, as regards spare poles lying on the ground within the take-off and landing areas or empty cups remaining on the wings. If the take-off or landing areas have become severely poached, do not hesitate to move the jump or ask an official to do so. The collecting ring can prove an alarming place for a young horse when it is very full and busy – always remember that the horse must never be allowed to become frightened.

The first few outings are usually quite exciting for the young horse and are certainly very tiring. When its companion returns to the box, both horses can be made comfortable and ready to travel, given a drink and a haynet and loaded. If the companion has other classes to do, the youngster can be allowed to graze on a lead rope rather than be left alone in the box. If there are several horses in the same lorry, the youngster can be left with them and its haynet. It must *never* be left alone.

This type of experience is extremely beneficial for the young horse in that, when the day finally arrives for it to compete, it will be used to the atmosphere, noise, bustle and crowds of a competition. There are various competitions in which horses can start their careers. I usually choose a small, unaffiliated dressage competition or a show class for my young horses. At a dressage competition, more than one class can usually be entered, so any mistakes that may be made at the first attempt can be corrected at the second.

Preparation is the secret of success, so plenty of time must be allowed for all the jobs at home prior to leaving. Allow plenty of time for the journey, plenty of time to collect the numbers, to identify the arena and, of greatest importance, plenty of time to ride-in. If there is plenty of time for everything the rider will feel more relaxed and the horse will be happier. When going to the horse's first show, allow at least half an hour longer to ride-in than would be necessary at home.

## USEFUL COMPETITIONS TO FURTHER THE EDUCATION OF THE YOUNG HORSE

Showing classes can assist in getting a young horse or pony accustomed to public display, be it in the ring, dressage arena or jumping classes. In the UK there is a variety of Riding Horse and Hunter classes, some of which include a jump. Those for the Working Hunter will include a course of rustic fences. If the intention is to enter a Working Hunter class, a note should be made of the dimensions of the obstacles that are going to be faced. At first you should only enter for the Novice classes, as the Open classes can be very big!

Many shows run Minimus jumping competitions at various heights. These classes are designed for training purposes. The competitor enters the ring, jumps a round and may collect a rosette if they go clear but can also pay for a second attempt if mistakes were made. The BSJA (British Show Jumping Association) organizes a progression of classes for young horses. These classes require that both horse and rider are registered with the BSJA. The show must also be affiliated to the association, which ensures that the courses are built to a recognized standard by experienced course builders using good fences.

A competitor in a Minimus show jumping class.

The same rules about allowing plenty of time apply equally to a dressage show or a jumping competition. The period of riding-in should be the same as that followed at the rehearsal 'parties', with only a few practice fences. Always try to be aware of the intentions of fellow competitors in the collecting ring so that your young horse is not upset by someone cutting across the fence at the last minute. At a properly run show, the practice fence will be flagged, as in the arena, with red on the right and white on the left, ensuring that the flow of traffic comes in the same direction. At less well-organized venues such precautions may be omitted. Not only is this extremely dangerous for the experienced horse and rider, it could also prove disastrous if the young horse were to meet another horse jumping the fence from the opposite direction at the same time. Confidence will be destroyed immediately.

## WALKING THE COURSE

At a jumping competition, the course must be carefully walked by the rider on foot, just as it will be jumped, from start to finish. When walking round, certain factors must be considered:

- the direction of the approach (whether it is towards the other horses/boxes or away);
- the position of the next fence (the severity of the turn);
- the condition of the ground (hard, good, deep or slippery – adjustments must be made so that the horse can remain balanced);
- the type of fence (a spooky type of fence, for example, a water tray or a brightly coloured filler, will need stronger riding);
- the distance between the fences in combinations or between jumps that are close enough to be on a related distance.

When first competing, the way in which the horse jumps the course is the most important thing, not winning. Once the horse has learnt to jump calmly and obediently, then it will be time to consider speed.

Remember to walk a jump-off course at the same time as you walk the full course. There will be no later opportunity to walk it should you be successful enough to qualify for the jump-off. Short cuts and opportunities to make sharp turns must all be decided upon in the initial walk round. Unless you are unlucky in the draw and have to go early in the jump-off, the tracks taken by other competitors should be observed and, perhaps, your plans will have to be altered according to their experiences. Competitions against the clock are won by crafty and often audacious turns and short cuts, not by galloping flat out.

During this introductory period, it must be remembered that, despite careful preparation, horses can have off days and are not machines. No one should become discouraged if success does not come straightaway but a positive analysis must be made of the performance. Both the good and the bad points must be noted so that the correct future programme can be worked out and training amended if necessary.

When jumping indoors, be very careful to maintain rhythm and balance around the course. There is a great temptation for the rider to overcheck the horse in the corners and turn its head outwards in an effort to gain more room for the turn. It is better to use your legs rather than the outside rein to negotiate a turn. All that turning the horse's head does is break its rhythm, upset its balance and prevent it from seeing the next obstacle! The horse must be ridden positively forward, with gentle curves at each corner. If the arena is too small for the horse to maintain a balanced canter, it is better to trot through any sharp turns.

For the event horse, the same introductory programme of dressage competitions and small show jumping classes is ideal.

A competitor in a Pre-novice class.

Cross-country training must also be included. Numerous practice courses can be hired for this purpose. It is advisable to take an experienced horse with you the first couple of times to give the young horse a lead, if necessary, at the more unusual fences.

In the UK, hunting or drag hunting offers a means of gaining experience across country, although with some packs the jumping is minimal. With all packs hunting is expensive and there is always a high risk to the horse.

The horse must be five years old before it can compete in a one day event. Riding clubs organize unaffiliated one day events at both Novice and Open level, which can provide a good starting platform. The BHS (British Horse Society) organizes a progression of horse trials, starting with Pre-novice. These, like the affiliated show jumping classes, are only open to horses and riders who are registered with the affiliating body, in this case the BHS. Again, the courses are built by trained course builders, using approved materials, and the courses are also inspected by an official BHS steward.

When jumping a cross-country course, either in a hunter trial or a one day event, the course must be carefully walked. The same rules as for walking a course of show jumps apply to the walking of the cross-country course, only with more emphasis on the terrain and weather conditions because the going and the gradient of the hills become vital factors. Ground that has been rotavated can cause problems by hiding holes or exposing stones. A course that includes successive drop fences will also cause stress and strain on the horse's front legs, especially if the landings have not been prepared with sand. Weather conditions can also affect the performance of the horse. In a hot or humid atmosphere, everyone must take precautions (see p.144).

Well-built cross-country courses will always have a suitable alternative at the difficult fences and careful walking of the course will include observation of all the alternatives. This enables the more novice horses to take an easier fence, which will involve a more time-wasting route, but will prevent it from being overfaced or frightened. As the horse becomes more experienced, it can then take the quicker routes. The correct use of alternatives should result in the majority of horses happily completing the course but still allow the best horses to win the rosettes.

## STRESS

Horses must be trained at home to cope with the stress that they will encounter at a competition. It must also be remembered that some horses love travelling and competing and some do not. Careful selection of the right horse and the right rider for each

Training over small, well-built cross-country fences is good preparation for one day events.

competition will help to reduce the stress factor for all concerned.

During training, the routine riding times should be altered every now and again so that the horse does not become upset at a competition if the class is not at its usual riding time. It is difficult enough for horses to relax in the atmosphere of a large show or event when other horses are going in and out of trailers and stables at all times, lights are left on and there are large crowds and a lot of noise, without allowing them to get upset about the riding time.

Horses are creatures of habit, so the riding-in pattern at a show should follow a similar routine to the work done at home. Spooky horses present the biggest problem for the trainer as they are unpredictable in the way they may react. The horse will gain confidence from the feel and contact of the rider's leg and hand, so it must be ridden forward to get it there. Once it is between the leg and hand, you must maintain the balance.

Large crowds and arenas can affect the horse and make it tense. Always keep it moving and occupy its mind with exercises to encourage it to relax. Never insist that it must stand still as this may increase tension.

Riders can also cause the horse unnecessary stress by trying too hard. They can increase the tension by niggling nervously with hand or leg, or both, until the horse ceases to listen. In situations like this the only thing to do is to stop, relax and start again. Nothing causes stress more than bad temper. There must be give and take on the part of both horse and rider – results come from technique and mutual trust, not force.

People have had a tremendous influence on the evolution of the horse and, because of this, we have a responsibility for its welfare. We must keep our horses under constant observation and never stop checking them visually and assessing their mental attitude. Too much stress can cause a horse to have a mental breakdown, resulting in nappiness, sullenness and an unwillingness to work. Alternatively, at the other end of the scale, they may rebel by becoming explosive, even to the point of attacking those who care for them by kicking and biting.

There are two extremes of attitude about putting stress and strain on the horse. It is obvious that horses not in heavy work do not suffer as much as those that are, especially if the work is boring or repetitive. Too much strain will break horses but putting horses under a certain amount of strain will also encourage the development of the species and encourage the proper type of horse to be bred.

What has to be decided is what is acceptable. The responsibility lies with the trainers, riders, course builders and rule makers of the various disciplines.

## SUITABILITY

The suitability of the horse for the job allocated to it will affect the amount of stress it is put under. Unsuitability will lead to extreme stress, while suitability for the chosen career will minimize stress and make problems less likely to occur. Several factors must be taken into account:

- breeding controls the potential performance. Progeny from non-competing parents need many stimuli to get them going. Foals will become interested in their surroundings and the activities taking place around their dams;
- physique – anatomy and conformation. The ratio between the body weight and the strength of the limbs is vital;
- metabolism – the horse's internal chemistry and energy factory;
- fitness and conditioning – different types of fitness are required for different disciplines and it is crucial that fittening is done properly;
- training – teaching the horse what is required in the performance;
- experience – it is important to progress slowly, one step at a time;
- action – the way in which the horse moves. Certain criteria are important for different disciplines. Power jumpers must have good angles in the joints of the hind leg and foreleg. Stayers must have straight limbs and economical strides. Event horses must strike a happy medium. Dressage horses must move well; the back must be neither too long nor too short and the branches of the jaw should be sufficiently wide to allow proper flexion at the poll;
- attitude – the horse must have a calm temperament and a good mental approach. Quiet horses are less likely to damage themselves;
- athletic ability – those horses that have this work within themselves and therefore cause themselves less damage.

The severity of competition will inevitably induce some failures but training should not. Stick fairly close to nature and do not think of horses being either human or like machines and training can be both successful and enjoyable.

## CARE OF THE HORSE AFTER A COMPETITION

After the horse has finished, the type of immediate care it receives will depend upon the activity that has been completed and the weather conditions. Hot and humid days are the worst and heavily muscled horses are less able to cope with these than their lighter, more wiry counterparts.

Endurance horses, eventers and racehorses should all receive thorough aftercare. They must be pulled up gradually at the finish and be kept between the rider's hand and leg to avoid strain on the muscles and tendons. The rider should dismount and loosen the surcingle and girth while the horse is still walking (removing the saddle itself if at a three day event or racing). The noseband can also be loosened and a sweat rug put over the horse's back. It can then be led back to either the stables or to the lorry or trailer. It must not stop walking until it has stopped blowing and its breathing has returned to normal.

On returning to the stables or the trailer, the horse should be thoroughly washed down. In very hot conditions, you can also rub ice under the tail, down the insides of the forearms and inside the thighs. Avoid putting water on the horse's back or hindquarters.

After washing down, scrape off the excess water and put on a sweat rug and roller. The number of rugs will depend on the weather and the discretion of the handler. The horse must continue walking until it is cool and dry.

The feet should be picked out, studs removed, if used, and stable bandages put on with Gamgee or Fibagee underneath, especially if the horse is going to travel. These will promote circulation and provide support for weary legs.

## Watering

The horse should be allowed a quarter of a bucket of water within 15 minutes of finishing, followed by a quarter of a bucket every 15 minutes thereafter. For endurance horses and eventers, it is advisable to give electrolytes before, during and after the competition. Horses will only drink these if they actually require them, so fresh water should also be made available. Then leave the horse to rest for an hour or so.

## Subsequent Care

The greater the strain under which the horse has competed, the longer the recovery period will be. For the dressage horse or show jumper, subsequent care can follow on almost immediately after the preliminaries. With the racehorse or eventer, these ministrations should be delayed. In hot conditions, all competing horses may require sponging down to remove excess sweat.

When the horse has returned to its stable, it must be gently groomed to remove sweat and checked for cuts or swellings. It can then have its rugs and some dry stable bandages put on. It should be given a small feed and some hay, followed later by its normal feed, when additional rugs may be necessary.

During the evening the horse must be checked again to ensure that it has not broken out in a sweat or become unsettled in any way. The water buckets must be replenished and possibly another feed and some extra hay given. The horse must then be left in peace to rest.

The following day it should be led out in hand and given some grass or turned out for a quiet, relaxing day in the field. It must be thoroughly groomed and checked over when it is brought in. Any lameness or abnormality must be treated and the advice of a veterinary surgeon possibly sought.

# POINTS TO REMEMBER

In this last chapter, I am in danger of repeating myself but my main object here is to emphasize points of special importance.

## FITNESS AT ALL AGES

Horses and ponies must be trained at home to cope with everything that they will encounter at a competition and that includes being produced at peak physical fitness for the discipline concerned. Success in anything is achieved by correct training and by paying attention to detail. The horse must be fit enough to do the task asked of it with minimum fatigue. Once your four-year-old has completed its early training and is ready to go on to 'grown-up' activities, you must make sure that you follow a proper fittening regime when you bring the horse back into work after time off.

Each discipline demands a different type of fitness from the horse and a horse that is fit for one activity may not be fit enough for another. Three months should be allowed to get the horse from soft condition to general hunting or one day event fitness, while a racehorse or three day event horse will need another month in which to reach its peak of physical and respiratory fitness. To obtain this fitness, a correct combination of work and feeding is necessary.

The first six weeks of any fittening programme will be the same and should include walk and slow trotting, starting with three-quarters of an hour's walking exercise and working up to two hours, including walk and trot. During this period the routine stable management tasks must be undertaken. Shoeing and worming must be done as soon as the horse comes in and the process should be repeated every six weeks thereafter. These essentials should be planned in advance so that they will not clash with any competitions later on. 'Flu and anti-tetanus vaccinations must be brought up to date with current competition rules and an entry made by the veterinary surgeon to this effect on the horse's passport. If these inoculations are given during the walking stage of the programme, they will not interrupt serious work later.

The horse's teeth should also be checked and should continue to be looked at by an equine dentist every six months. If there are any abnormalities in the mouth, they may need attention at more regular intervals. Some competition and racing yards also take a blood test before any serious work begins, to check that the horse is in good condition. Finally, thorough grooming and careful feeding are essential to enable the horse to reach its full potential.

After the initial six weeks of basic fittening, specialist training may commence and a choice can be made of how to proceed with the fittening regime.

A well-developed dressage horse, reflecting years of training.

Two types of fitness programme are used by competitors. The first is the traditional method and the second is called interval training. Both will get the horse fit if carried out properly. The traditional method includes long periods of work, eventually building up to cantering for 12 minutes. During the last month, the canter work decreases in distance but increases in speed.

Interval training was first developed in Scandinavia for human athletes and was later adapted for horses. It consists of measured periods of work and measured intervals of rest and therefore puts less strain on the limbs of the horses. Precise records must be made of the horse's pulse and respiratory rate at the end of each period of work and the length of time it takes it to regain normal rates of pulse and respiration to determine its stage of fitness. The shorter the length of time it takes for the pulse and respiration to return to normal, the greater is the horse's degree of fitness. It is, of course, essential to know the normal pulse and respiratory rates of the individual horse when at rest before work begins.

## SOUNDNESS

Before starting any fitness programme the soundness of the horse must be considered. Any horse can become unsound through injury but those that have shortcomings in their conformation are more susceptible than those that do not.

As a general rule, horses must move straight. Not only must the hind legs follow in the tracks of the front legs, thus making it

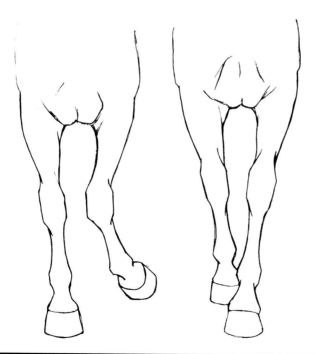

Dishing and plaiting.

possible for 'straightness' to occur on a circle, but also there should be no deviation from the perpendicular in any of the four limbs nor in the action of those limbs when viewed from the front or rear. *Dishing* with either of the front legs occurs when the lower part of the limb swings in an outward motion before coming to the ground. This action puts strain on all the joints in that limb and will probably result in lameness at a later date. *Brushing* is where one foot knocks against the opposite leg and is also detrimental. Boots can be used on the horse for protection but they are not practical in some disciplines, while in others they are actually prohibited. *Plaiting*, when one foreleg crosses in front of the other, can be particularly dangerous when galloping.

These are all visible deficiencies that can be observed by an unqualified person but there may be other deficiencies in conformation or health that are best discerned by a veterinary surgeon. It is essential that the young horse is physically fit and able to perform correctly throughout its education. An old saying goes, 'You cannot make a silk purse out of a sow's ear' and to try to break and school an animal that is physically incapable of carrying out the tasks asked of it is not only frustrating and a waste of time and money but could, in extreme cases, lead to discomfort for the pupil if not actually inflicting cruelty upon it.

The eye of the horse is the window of its soul. The one that looks straight back at the observer with trust and honesty is the one with which to persevere. However, there are also many horses that have been mollycoddled and pampered, so a happy medium must be found between spoiling and too much discipline for the horse to be happy.

Today, when the human race is increasing the pace of life to such an extent that good manners and civility seem, sadly, a thing of the past, we must not forget to ask the horse politely for anything that is required. An animal that is not treated with the respect it deserves is most likely to reflect this through its training by ignoring the aids and being unpleasant to ride. This book has tried to explain the value of systematic training from foal to adult horse.

The importance of handling the foal has been fully described in the early chapters. The basis of successful training is the formation of trust between horse and human and this must be established from the very beginning.

## GENERAL GUIDELINES OF PROGRESSION

The breaking-in process starts with handling and the introduction to various experiences of the foal and young horse. By the time the horse is in its third summer it is usually considered the right time

to start training in preparation for backing. Once the horse has accepted a rider sitting on its back, more sophisticated training can begin.

*Above* In the first six months, the horse should be taught the basic aids.

## During the First Six Months

The horse should be worked on large circles, equally on each rein, and should learn about transitions. In the latter half of this period, canter can be introduced, initially on straight lines and for short distances. The object of these first lessons in canter is to achieve a smooth transition without excitement and any refinements, such as the correct leading leg, will come later. The horse is taught the meaning of the aids. The inside rein is for steering; the outside rein controls the speed and offers some balance to the young horse. The rider's inside leg creates and maintains inpulsion and moves the horse into the outside rein. The rider's outside leg is principally concerned with control of the hindquarters.

*Opposite* During the 6 to 12-month period of training, the horse becomes more established in its work.

During this period the horse must be ridden out on hacks and can start work over poles or cavaletti. Whether the work is being carried out in an arena or out on a hack, the rider must always sit centrally and ride forward. By this I mean that, even when asking for downward transitions or halt, the rider must be thinking forward, not pulling back.

It is also important that the rider indulges in positive thinking and thinks of the result required instead of anticipating what may go wrong. With positive thinking, aids may very well become automatic and natural. Where anxious anticipation intervenes, the subconscious reaction of a rider who is anticipating problems or dangers can transmit itself to the horse and be misinterpreted, thus producing exactly the opposite effect to the reaction desired. Two obvious examples of this are traffic shyness – where the rider is the one who is traffic shy and tenses up – or breaking from one gait to another, usually in upward transitions in a dressage test.

## The Next Six to Twelve Months of Training

If the basic work is proceeding in a satisfactory manner, further training can be introduced, such as the increase and decrease of pace within the gait and the art of halting. When the horse starts to anticipate halt at a certain place, this is an ideal time to teach the half-halt. Once rhythm and balance have been established, the large circles in trot can be made smaller. Canter circles and the lengthening and shortening of the canter stride also need practice. The rider should start to sit up and use their seat and back to slow the horse down, rather than causing any antagonism through the rein. The polework will progress to jumping small obstacles of varying types. Gymnastic exercises will also help to make the horse more supple and athletic as well as making it more alert mentally.

## After Eighteen Months of Training

The horse must start to move away from the rider's leg so that lateral work can be developed. Jumpers and eventers must be capable of lengthening and shortening the stride with no argument. Most horses that progress further than Novice level should work towards Medium standard in dressage. This applies not only to event horses but will also prove extremely helpful for show jumpers and show ponies or even the hunter. Progress cannot be hurried; the standard will not be reached in under a year.

During the period of basic training, the young horse can be turned out and, in that first year, need not be ridden every day. It must also be given holidays at applicable times so that it has time to relax both mentally and physically. Spring grass is also essential for the development of the young horse. Attention must be paid to the length of these 'holidays'. Too long a period at grass will be detrimental to both physical and mental fitness. A balance must be struck between a period that is long enough to allow for mental relaxation and access to good grass but not so long as to subject the animal to boredom, torment from flies, scarcity of good grazing or severe weather conditions. Remember, the rest is for the benefit of the horse not the convenience of the rider!

## OVERFACING

It is vital at every stage throughout training that the horse is never overfaced. This applies to the work it is asked to do both on the flat and over fences. All training must be carried out in a logical sequence so that the horse has a solid foundation on which to build its experience.

If a problem occurs, the trainer must be willing to go back to a stage in training that the horse understands so that it can accomplish the task with which it has been presented without tension or anxiety. This will help to rebuild the horse's confidence and its ability to advance. If the basic tenets have been firmly established, the horse should have a greater chance of understanding the progressively more demanding work required of it. Horses have exceptionally long memories and will easily relate and respond to earlier, less-demanding lessons.

## BOREDOM AND STABLE VICES

Boredom can become quite a problem if the horse is left standing in the stable for long periods. The same can be the result of too long a holiday period, especially in the dry summer months when the grass is sparse.

### Weaving
This name is given to a nervous disorder in which the horse, while stationary, will swing its head and neck from side to side. It stands with its front legs apart but, in severe cases, these may even be lifted off the ground as the horse sways from side to side.

Although weaving is usually a result of boredom, it can be copied from another horse that weaves in the same yard. In some cases a foal can learn to weave if its mother is a weaver. Weaving is technically an unsoundness and has to be declared at the time of any sale. It is not a physical unsoundness, however, except that it obviously puts unnecessary stress and strain on the joints of the front limbs. It also denotes a degree of nervous tension in the mind of the horse.

## Crib-biting and Windsucking

Crib-biting starts with the horse chewing wood. In its early stages, this practice is mildly detrimental to the horse's digestion, especially if the wood has been painted. The real danger, however, is the wearing down of the teeth which, in turn, impares the efficiency of the initial process of digestion, i.e. the grinding of the food as it mixes with saliva. Even more important is the fact that crib-biting leads to windsucking.

A windsucker gulps air at the same time as it bites on the top of the door, projecting manger, etc. The habit becomes more and more intense and the confirmed windsucker will even do this against its own foreleg or, when lying down, against the floor. Various devices have been produced to counteract this practice, such as straps around the gullet or perforated, hollow bits in the mouth but these devices are seldom effective.

To prevent the initial stages of crib-biting, a metal strip or a grille over the top of the door is to be recommended. Similar grilles can also be effective in the case of weaving. Raw, unseasoned wood, especially if it still contains sap, is more attractive to the miscreant than wood treated with a preservative such as creosote. If paint is used, it should be of the lead-free variety. Most preservatives are noxious, so time must be allowed for them to penetrate the wood and to dry and any surplus should be wiped off the surfaces before occupancy of the stable is resumed.

Crib-biting and windsucking are both nervous habits that can develop through boredom or be copied from a companion and both must be disclosed at the time of sale if the horse is warranted sound. Horses that windsuck very often develop 'pot bellies' due to the excess air in their stomachs.

Once these stable vices are adopted, they are incurable and their presence greatly reduces the value of the horse. As in everything, prevention is better than cure. Keep the programme of work varied and, if possible, turn the horse out in a paddock for a couple of hours each day. During inclement weather, a New Zealand rug should be put on the clipped horse and, in extreme weather, extra rugs put on underneath this, to keep the horse warm. With a young horse, that is not going to be subjected to exceptionally demanding physical tasks, a blanket or trace clip will prove more practical than a full hunter clip.

When the horse is in its stable, it should be given a haynet so that it has something to occupy itself with while it is confined.

Some years ago a 'complete nut' was developed by one of the leading food manufacturers. It was intended to take the place of both the concentrate ration and the bulk ration of the horse's diet. The initial reason for producing this so-called 'complete nut' was that the British equine teams travelling to the Mexico Olympic

A windsucker. The horse has got hold of the door and is gulping in air at the same time.

A contented horse, eating from its haynet in the stable.

Games considered available local feedstuffs to be of inferior quality. They required a complete food that was less bulky to transport than conventional feedstuffs.

Although this product was proclaimed as a brand-new innovation by the manufacturers, this proved to be untrue. During the Second World War, the German army relied extensively on horse transport during the Russian campaign and these animals had to be fed. Because of the policy of 'scorched earth', as they retreated all feeding stuffs had to be carried vast distances by train to reach the fighting areas, so German nutrition scientists produced the complete nut. This saved hundreds of train journeys.

The complete nut proved a success and no problem was observed in the performance or behaviour of the hard-worked animals consuming them. Similarly, the British Olympic equestrians had a successful experience with the feeding of this substitute. However, some months after their return to the UK, when asked whether they were still feeling the complete food, most, if not all, admitted that they were not. Despite this, commercial introduction on to the general market was made and many horse owners experimented in their own stables. In most cases the experiment was not a success. Why?

The answer was the amount of work required of the recipients and the amount of time spent with nothing to do. The German army horses were being worked to the point of exhaustion. They had no time to be bored. The same applied, to a degree, to horses in the last stages of preparation for Olympic competition or while actually competing. Although not worked to exhaustion, they were fully occupied during a large part of the day. The private horse, spending, as it does, hours each day doing nothing in the stable, can become so bored that it develops stable vices and a belligerent attitude towards those looking after it. It could even become dangerous. Consequently, the importance of the haynet cannot be overstressed.

## DIET

The diet for the young horse is just as important as the diet for any young animal that is still developing. It is vital that it receives all the necessary vitamins and minerals in order to develop correctly. If the youngster is being fed a compound mix or nut specially designed for young horses, this should provide a balanced ration containing all the necessary vitamins and minerals, especially copper. This micro-nutrient is essential for the successful production of bone from cartilage in the young animal. Without it, certain deformities, such as cow hocks and enlarged joints, can occur. The composition of the ration is worked out by a nutritionist and each ingredient is carefully analysed for quality before mixing so that you can be assured that the horse is receivng all that it requires. In addition to the concentrate diet, hay is fed on an ad lib basis, thus providing additional bulk to aid digestion and a pastime that will occupy the stabled horse. Always remember that the horse must be fed according to its size, type, temperament and the amount of work being done. The diet should contain plenty of protein while it is still growing but very little carbo-hydrate, so that the horse does not become too excitable. This is especially true for ponies.

While we often hear distressing reports of malnutrition due to the provision of insufficient or unsuitable feeding stuffs, the effects of overfeeding are not so much highlighted. Many an over-fat, over-indulged hack or hunter suffers from obesity. Broken wind is only one of the results of this over-indulgence. A prime example is the hunter turned out in lush pasture and brought into fast work too quickly in early autumn. At the other end of the scale, too much spring grass can lead to laminitis and, eventually, dropped soles, especially in ponies. Many dressage horses or eventers have been over-indulged in their owners' desire to produce extrava-gance of action in the dressage arena or as a preparation for the endurance phases of combined training. Many inexperienced trainers look to the fancy bits and appliances on the loriner's shelves to restrain the exuberance of their over-energized horses. A more simple solution, in stark, old-fashioned terms, would be to 'cut their oats'. It is also cheaper.

A prize makes all the hard work worth while!

# INDEX